P9-ARH-378

Toward an Adult Faith

*I would like to
sum it up this way.
God for us is
life giver and lover.
God sent Jesus to be
life giver and lover.
Jesus did a good job
of it. Jesus now sends
his church to be
life giver and lover.
That means us.*

9857

Eugene A. Walsh

Toward an Adult Faith

TALKING ABOUT THE BIG QUESTIONS

With Reflections about Gene Walsh by
TOM CONRY AND VIRGIL C. FUNK

OCP Publications

Cover design: Jean Germano

© 1994, OCP Publications. All rights reserved.
5536 N.E. Hassalo, Portland, OR 97213-3638
1-800-LITURGY (548-8749)
Printed in the United States of America

ISBN 0-915531-23-2

Contents

Acknowledgments

Oregon Catholic Press is happy to present the complete works of Eugene A. Walsh, S.S.

We are honored to be able to continue his pioneering ministry in liturgy and spirituality.

We thank those who helped prepare these volumes in memory of their dear friend and teacher Gene Walsh:

Ruth Eger
Fred J. Nijem
Elaine Rendler
Virgil C. Funk
James Hansen
Tom Conry
and many others

Complete Works of Eugene A. Walsh

Spirituality: Christian Life in the World Today
Giving Life: Ministry of the Parish Sunday Assembly
Assembly Edition
Giving Life: Ministry of the Parish Sunday Assembly
Leader's Guide
Celebration: Theology, Ministry and Practice
Proclaiming God's Love in Word and Deed
Proclaiming God's Love in Song
Toward an Adult Faith: Talking about the Big Questions

To all of you
who have helped make me,
those present,
those already gone.
You have touched me.
You know who you are.
I know who you are.
I have touched you.
We both know that.
I hold you deep in my heart.
I cherish you dearly.
I love you.
Keep holding me.
Don't let me go.
Through you, with you, in you,
I have found God.
But more, through you and me,
with you and me, in you and me,
God found us all forever.

It was he who appointed some to be apostles,
others to be prophets, others to be evangelists,
others to be pastors and teachers
as a service for all God's people
to build up the body of Christ.

So we shall all come together to that oneness in our faith,
and in our knowledge of the Son of God,
we shall become mature people,
reaching to Christ's full stature.

Let us, therefore, no longer be children,
carried by waves and blown around by all winds of teaching
that comes out of human trickery to lead others astray.

Instead,
let us speak truth in love
and grow up to maturity in Christ the head.
Through him the whole body grows
and all the members fit together.
When each member works as it should,
the whole body builds itself up through love.

— Ephesians 4:11–16

Introduction

This book is for adults only, particularly for those Catholic adults who go to Mass every Sunday. This book is my response to a question that has been nagging at me for years: What do believing Catholics and other Christians need to know — about God and Jesus and the Spirit, about sin and reconciliation and about other truths of their faith — in order to survive and grow in their world of faith and worship and daily living?

Put it another way. What do adults need to know about these basic truths that they could not learn as children? The teaching of religion, catechism, whatever you wish to call it, is precisely and carefully designed for children. It has to be, because children are not adults and cannot sustain adult fare. There have been great advances in the area of elementary and high school religion teaching, both in content and process. But let's face it: it is still "kid stuff." It is not adequate for adults.

Yet the majority of adults have had to make do with this fare throughout all their lives. Except for those who moved on into college and perhaps graduate school, the average churchgoer was doomed to make his or her way into the adult world lacking the insights that alone could help them survive and grow. Even college teaching was often a rehash of what students had already learned somehow at the primary and secondary level. They were bored, and rightly so. I realize that there are all kinds of factors that make religion boring to adolescents and young adults. I do know, however, from much experience, that a large part of the problem is the seeming irrelevance of the material. Like clothing, it was supposed to fit but didn't. So, as with clothing that does not fit, it was discarded.

To compound the problem, average Sunday preaching is not nourishing in style, mode or content. I am not saying anything new. Everybody who cares in the least is talking about the poor quality of Sunday preaching. If anything, I am saying it in a more careful and contained way. There is an admitted crisis of preaching in the church today. Andrew M. Greeley's research found it to be a major cause for priests' loss of credibility. A recent document from the Bishops' Committee on Priestly Life and Ministry has this to say:

> "Preaching is increasingly becoming an area of concern and intense study. Research has shown a growing disenchantment among the people with the quality of preaching. Magazine articles critical of preaching appear with disturbing regularity. The matter is complex and related surely to many factors."
> — *As One Who Serves: Reflections on the Pastoral Ministry of Priests in the United States* (1977), #42.

This statement about preaching is a nice way of saying that the average Sunday Mass homily is dull and not worth listening to. It states that the matter is "complex" and "related surely to many factors." Two of these factors are clear and certain: communication and content. Too many preachers are not saying anything worth adult listening, and they are not saying it well. Too many of those who are preaching reasonably adult fare are not saying it in clear, understandable language. There is too much untranslated theological jargon aimed at an upper middle class college and university level. Often preachers do not understand it either.

Whatever the exact reasons, the situation is like the story told about the two elderly Vermonters at a political rally in their small town. One of the local contenders was carrying on from the soap box. After a bit, one of the gentlemen, who was hard of hearing, leaned over to his companion and asked: "What's that feller up there talking about?" "He don't say," shouted his companion.

Adults cannot make it through life on childhood fare. Those adults who continue on with what they got as children, remain children. They do not grow up. We have lots of evidence for that. On the other hand, many adults discover that the knowledge they gained as children and adolescents does not sustain them in their struggle to survive in an adult world. It does not help them deal effectively with the many adult questions and crises they are facing all the time. Nobody tries for long to do a job with tools that do not work.

I return to my original question: What do adults need to know to live as adults in this complex world? What do they need to know in order to live in the world and the church *today?*

Today means this particular moment in history that has been fashioned both inside and outside the church by the break-through work of scripture scholars, theologians, liturgists and catechists. The careful and insightful work of these scholars demanded a council and, at the same time, provided the stuff of the council's reform and renewal. Their work makes it possible and necessary for all Christians to see again in a fresh and exciting way the vision of God's loving, saving presence among his people through Jesus and through the church.

Today means the beginning of what looks like a new age in the church, a new age dawning after more than a thousand years. It means that our present time is one in which people with vision are asking what will be the shape of the church within the next few decades.

Today means the time in God's life-giving plan that is given to us, to all adults, to work with God in making the path straight for the heavenly reign. The coming to fullness of God's plan depends on us as well as on God. Today, then, is the privilege and responsibility of all adults. We have the power to make God's plan become alive and life-giving.

The great news is that we are getting more adults in the church today who can do the job and who want to do the job of making the church come alive as a sign and instrument of God's reign. By baptism we are called directly by Jesus to be disciples of the good news. This role of discipleship is not, as was thought for a long time, the work of the hierarchy. It is the job of all adult members of the church. That is the only qualification: to be an adult.

If we would try to put a nametag on our age in the church today we would have to call it "the age of adults." It is no longer "children's hour." It is "adult hour" in the whole world as well as in the church. The vast and sometimes violent upheaval in third world countries and the grass roots energy of change in the church is generated mainly by individuals and a people coming of age.

This coming of age of people in the world is the biggest thing that is happening in our time. All over, adults forced to live like children are in rebellion. They are claiming — even more, they are demanding — adult status in that part of the world in which they live. In many respects the revolution is soundless and bloodless but no less effective.

Those who are mounting this revolution share the same voice. The cry is simple and clear. "We are adults, not children, and we will no longer tolerate being treated as children. We are bent on claiming again our first-class citizenship in the church. It is our birthright in the city of God."

It is a new exodus. From all sides they come marching from the authoritarian servitude of many religious communities, from rectories and convents, from unquestioned parental authority, from paternalistic government. Many adults are choosing to leave the structures that oppress them and force them to live and behave as children. A large number are choosing to stay but they have grown up. They are demanding that the patterns and structures be changed to suit adults and the way adults live.

There are many signs: People all over the world stopped going to confession the old way, which was the way of a child. The departure of women religious from religious life was due, more than to any other cause, to their refusal to live any longer as children. So it was for the large number of priests who left their ministry. The issue for many of them was very much, but not altogether, the issue of celibacy. Whimsical and capricious exercise of authority played a goodly part in that exodus.

Whatever the choice, those who are mounting this revolution share the same voice. The cry is simple and clear. "We are adults, not children, and we will no longer tolerate being treated as children. We are bent on claiming again our first-class citizenship in the church. It is our birthright in the city of God. No one in authority has the right to dictate the way in which we live, the choices we make, the decisions we alone are able to make. No one has the right to take away our God-given freedom as grown-up persons."

The days of so-called blind obedience are gone. The principle was never valid. No one has the right to such obedience except God. God, most of all, does not demand it. God respects the freedom of people. God expects people to go about the difficult business of forming their consciences, making their decisions and sticking to them.

The struggle is on and will continue for a long time. People in power, no matter who they are or where they are, will do most anything to hold on to position and privilege. This is a universal phenomenon. It admits of almost no exceptions.

In this ongoing revolution of adults claiming their place in the sun, we are discovering the seeds of the church of the future. The church of the twenty-first century will not just happen. People will make it to be what it becomes. Fortunately for the generations to come, there are enough adults coming alive in the church today to give great hope and promise for the church of the next millennium.

All the materials that I have written and continue to write are geared for adults in today's church. To put it as bluntly as I can, I think we have a high level of ignorance in our church today. I would say that only a minority of church members have a clear idea of what it means to belong to church in the wake of Vatican II renewal.

What is the church for? What is the church's main task in the world? What is the church? How can we describe it best? More than that, how can we bring it to life? These are the major questions that adults must ask. They need to get sufficiently clear answers so that they can help the church of the twenty-first century become what it can be and ought to be.

I have written various materials to help us in this large and important task. They are materials that can be used in a parish. They are not written to be published and then placed on a bookshelf. They are not for the specialist but are meant to be used by all members of the assembly. They contain the theology of the renewed church and all the know-how to help in the process of bringing a parish to full life-giving ministry.

This revised version of "Talking with Adults" is part of that design. It is written for adult members of the parish. I have been told that the earlier version has served as a catalyst for genuine conversion for adults who had lost their way, had given up on the church, were confused and wanted very much to experience the saving love of God through Jesus. I am hoping that this second version will be of even greater help. Try it and see. They begin to live calmly and productively within the faith maturing process.

PART 1

Talking with Adults

1
THE CHURCH

What do adults today need to know about the church so that they can live as grown-up and responsible adults in the church? Amazingly few churchgoing Catholics know what it means to belong to the church. This is one of the greatest forms of ignorance in the church in our time.

To answer that question, we need to ask even more basic questions. We must ask the kind of questions for which we think we already have the answers. What exactly is the task of the church? What is the church supposed to be doing in the world? Are the local parish churches really doing the job they are called to do? Are our inherited, comfortable notions about the parish really valid notions?

If we look at our parishes today in light of Vatican II, we are going to get some surprising answers to these questions. It is becoming clearer and clearer now that the call of Vatican II is no routine thing. It is a call to the church for conversion, deep conversion, profound change such as we have not experienced for a thousand years. All this is simply because the council is calling the church to recover its original mission, to heed again the mandate given by Jesus to his first community of disciples: Go out! Don't stay at home. Go out! Proclaim the good news to those who have not heard. Live the gospel message as a sign to the whole world. Let your first concern be service to brothers and sisters.

Our task is to discover this mission of the church in the world, to celebrate it and to experience it until it gets into our hearts as well as into our heads. This task is the responsibility of the whole church and not that of just a few church leaders. We are the church. We, all of us adults, are held responsible. We had better do our job. The stakes are high.

Our first question is this: What is the church for? Why does the church exist? What is the job of the church in the world today? At parish level most Catholics believe, consciously or unconsciously, that the church, their parish, exists to serve the needs of those who belong to the parish, particularly those who come to church regularly. If you examine this notion carefully you come up with the idea that the parish is a sort of club that exists to serve the needs of those who belong.

This popular notion includes the idea that a parish has some responsibility also for the people who live within the parish bounds: churched, multi-churched or unchurched. This idea exists, however, only as a kind of canonical ideal. In reality, most of the energy and resources go to serve only those who do come. The pittance in the poor box is a silent witness to this fact. Only the leftovers go outside the parish; the same for clothing and food collections, praiseworthy as they are. In most parishes, priests and people operate on this unquestioned, unexpressed and unexamined premise that the parish exists for itself, for its members. Parishes showing a large sense of responsibility to the outside community are a decided minority.

I am stating a fact, not making an indictment. This self-contained, inner-directed concept of parish does prevail and has prevailed for some centuries. It has a long history of practice and theology to back it up. It is not my purpose here to study that history or that theology. I simply ask you to make an honest testing of your own experience. I urge you, as an adult, to ask some important questions.

Where does your parish money go? People always put their money on the things they value the most. What part of the parish budget goes for social justice? What is the outreach of the parish to the neighboring community? How many ministries are there to the sick, the poor, the elderly, the disadvantaged, those in prison? I mean ministries not just to the needy who belong to the parish, but to the needy wherever they are discovered. Is food regularly available for the hungry? Or do they know from experience that the parish is the place from which they are most likely to be turned away? Are there regular parish structures, maintained by regular parish money, that go out and look for the needy in order to help them?

Are these kinds of demands considered to have a claim on parish resources, both people and money, at least equal to the claim of parish programs, school, buildings? What regular and initiative-taking collaboration exists with other religious or civic agencies that provide care, concern and helping services to those in need?

What impact does the parish have on the neighborhood and the larger community of which it is a part? Do the neighborhood people even know that you exist apart from the presence of a church building? Does your presence make any real difference in the neighborhood? If a walk through your neighborhood reveals that the neighbors do not regard you as an important member of the community, your parish is in trouble.

Against this prevailing notion of an inner-directed and self-contained church stands the gospel notion of church clarified by the documents of Vatican II. After more than twenty years, we are beginning to understand that the reforms of Vatican II, if taken seriously, are radical indeed. The council does not ask merely that we rearrange the furniture in the old church. The council demands that we take a completely fresh look at what the church is for and what the church is.

We grew up in a world that understood church primarily as hierarchy: pope, bishops, presbyters, people, in either ascending or descending order — from me to the priest to God to the priest to me. This was the model almost everyone operated on. It was our most usual experience and understanding of church.

While the council does not completely abandon this model, which is basically a model of church order, it clearly proclaims that this inherited model is not adequate. The council demands that this model be brought to fullness of life by the addition of other models.

After more than twenty years, we are beginning to understand that the reforms of Vatican II, if taken seriously, are radical indeed. The council does not ask merely that we rearrange the furniture in the old church. The council demands that we take a completely fresh look at what the church is.

The Dogmatic Constitution on the Church gives us fresh images by which we are to understand the nature of the church and its mission to the world. It is important to note that these are not new images. These images reflect living realities of the church that got lost or set aside during the last millennium.

The image of the church as "people of God" comes to us as new. The image of the church as pilgrim and servant is also fresh and exciting. The image of the church as a community "sent" into the world to proclaim and witness the good news of God's saving love for all people — this is an exciting and close-to-gospel look. It is perhaps the most demanding of all images. It challenges at its core the prevailing notion of self-serving church.

These images of the church, if we take them seriously, are asking us to turn the church around, nothing less. They are calling us to make our own again the full mandate of Jesus to his disciples, the mandate that spells out the full mission of the church: Go out, proclaim the good news to everyone, serve brothers and sisters everywhere, no matter where they are, That is the full task of the church — the task, therefore, of every adult member of the church without exception.

The main ideas from Vatican II about the self-understanding of the church today tend to sort themselves out in the following manner. First, God's plan of salvation, the saving action of Jesus, is for all people at all times in all places. There are no "special" people for whom Jesus suffered and died and was raised up. No church has a monopoly on God's saving action.

All this (God's plan to save people through Jesus) holds true not only for Christians, but for all people of good will in whose hearts grace works in an unseen way. For, since Christ died for all people and since the ultimate vocation of people is, in fact, one and divine, we ought to believe that the Holy Spirit, in a manner known only to God, offers to every person the possibility of being associated with this paschal mystery. (cf. Pastoral Constitution on Church in the Modern World, 22)

The story goes something like this: when he died and was raised from the dead, Jesus sent the Spirit of God, now his own Spirit, into the whole world to bring God's life and love to all people. It is important to note that Jesus sent his Spirit into the whole world, not just into the church. We Catholics kind of grew up with the idea that Jesus' Spirit was the private possession of the church and the church alone. It was as if the church had a monopoly on the Spirit and was the only instrument of the Spirit in the world.

This is not so. The Spirit of Jesus is no more alive and active in the church than anywhere else in the world. The Spirit moves in whatever way the Spirit chooses. We cannot put bonds or limits on a totally free God. No one can.

The difference, then, between the church and all other people is that the church "knows." The community called church knows God's plan because God has revealed it to that community. The church community finds its place in God's plan to save all people in all ages by the simple but startling fact that God has revealed his plan to the church. The church "knows" what God is doing in all human creation and history because God told it so through Jesus in the power of the Spirit. That is why Juan Segundo suggests that the church can be simply described as "those who know" (in *The Community Called Church;* Maryknoll, NY: Orbis Books, 1973).

This is what the word "revelation" means. Jesus "revealed" God's plan of salvation to the church. The writer of Ephesians, in the spirit of Paul, says it well to the early church:

"In all his wisdom and insight God did what he had purposed, and made known to us the secret plan he had already decided to complete by means of Christ. This plan, which God will complete when the time is right, is to bring all creation together, everything in heaven and on earth, with Christ as head." (Ephesians 1:9–10)

This is the privilege of the church, and a mighty privilege it is. To know God's plan of saving love for all people is indeed a privilege. It is like getting an "inside tip," directly from Jesus, about God's plans for saving all people.

But with the privilege goes a great responsibility. Jesus gave this "inside tip" about God's plans to the church precisely so that members of the church would spread it around. Jesus charged his disciples to get out and proclaim this good news to all people. He charged them to be active sign and witness of God's saving presence in the world, to be, like himself, servant for all people.

This is the mission of the church, the job of the church in the world. By the action of Jesus the church has been formed and sent into the world to be a conscious and deliberate partner in God's saving work for all people.

"Like a pilgrim, the Church presses forward amid the persecutions of the world and the consolations of God, announcing the cross and death of the Lord until he comes." (Dogmatic Constitution on the Church, 8)

The council fathers are also explicit that no one is exempt from this responsibility.

"In our times a special obligation binds us to make ourselves neighbor to absolutely all persons and to give them active assistance when they come across our path." (Pastoral Constitution on the Church in the Modern World, 27)

All members of the church are called to discipleship directly, not through the instrumentality of the hierarchy. Jesus did not mandate bishops and priests first, who in turn mandated the rest of the church. The people's responsibility for the mission of the church is direct and immediate.

It is important to stress this idea because until quite recently the basic assumption of church mission was that Jesus entrusted the church's mission to the hierarchy, and only to the hierarchy. (Cf. Leonard Doohan, *The Lay-Centered Church*. Minneapolis: The Winston Press, Inc.)

This notion of the indirect discipleship of "non-ordained" people in the church is still pretty much alive in the thinking of a large number of people. The initiative of Vatican II breaks through this mold of thinking to declare that all people in the church, by reason of their membership in the church, share directly in the full mission of Christ, the full mission of the church.

Says the Dogmatic Constitution on the Church, "The apostolate of the laity is a sharing in the salvific mission of the Church. Through Baptism and Confirmation all are appointed to this apostolate by the Lord himself." (33)

Very literally, Jesus sends the whole church:

"All the People of God, as we have seen, share in the mission and ministry of the Church, and in the priesthood of Jesus Christ. Each person has been given special gifts by the Holy Spirit. The reception of these gifts brings with it the right and duty to use them for the service of one another and all people." (*As One Who Serves*. Washington, DC: USCC, 1977; 33)

The first reason for the existence of the church is to *go out,* to proclaim the good news that God loves all people without reservation or discrimination and means to save them all if they will receive his love. The first function of the church is to be a sign of God's love, of Jesus' saving action, and to serve all sisters and brothers everywhere, outside as well as inside.

The church is not like other organizations founded only to serve their own members. It is a community "sent" to those who are outside. All the activity of a parish, the energy of worship and education and service, does not have as its final purpose the needs of the members of the parish. All the activity and energy of a parish, if rightly directed, is ordered finally to help the parish community become a community of faith and service for all with whom they come in contact. Failing this, the parish simply flunks its most important testing.

Parish as a community sent out . . . parish as a sign of God's love for all . . . parish as servant, as pilgrim: these are the operative images today. This is the gospel image of church.

If this is the true image of church, then we have a big job to do and it is time to get going. It is time to turn the church around. It is time for conversion, real conversion, deep conversion.

This task of conversion is a big one. We must not underestimate it. The church is calling for no less than an almost complete "about face" from its members. We are not exactly experiencing overwhelming success in our efforts to make it happen.

It is safe to say that ninety percent of us churchgoing people do not tend to think of ourselves as disciples who are sent out to be witnesses and instruments of God's saving work in the world.

Most of us: dioceses, parishes, religious communities, know ourselves to be basically inner-directed and self-serving. This self-serving stance can be carried out with great care and compassion, and with good attention to all the principles of worship and basic pastoral care, but it is still turned inward.

This is simply a statement of fact, not a placing of blame.

Despite this fact, there are exciting signs of this conversion. Already, many people are getting the idea that there is more to being a Catholic than going to Mass on Sundays and keeping their individual noses clean. The word is getting out that it is time for a change.

We are witnessing signs of this conversion at all levels of the church. The signs are contained in the church's official call for all members to get involved in the activity called "evangelization." Evangelization is a word in our active vocabulary right now. It is being urged upon us at international, national, diocesan and parish levels.

The first reason for the existence of the church is to give life. The church has been called to take the place of Jesus in the world. The first business of church, therefore, is to be life giver for all people.

More importantly, the term "evangelization" is no longer telling church members to go out and make people into Catholics. It is sending out a different signal: let all the people, both in the church and outside, know that we who call ourselves "church" really care about them and stand ready to serve them in any way that we can. There is no price to pay. There are no gimmicks, no traps, no contracts to sign, no effort to proselytize. Just proclaim, it, live it, and let the Spirit of Jesus work his power. All this has the healthy ring of gospel good news.

What is the good news we are to proclaim? It bears repeating, bears being shouted out again and again: God loves all people! God sent Jesus to make known his love, to gather people together and to bring them back to him! Jesus came and did the task he was sent to do. Jesus is risen now and is with us. He is alive and actively present in the whole world through the power of the Spirit, revealing, loving, gathering, bringing back. Jesus is alive in the whole universe, in all people everywhere, not just in a chosen and easy-to-identify few. In the church and through the church, Jesus can be recognized and proclaimed for all to know. Church members, therefore, know themselves as "in service," as was Jesus himself, to all people in order to help make God's glorious reign come!

Evangelization takes its cue from this notion of church captured from the gospels, captured from the apostolic church, captured and held again in the theology and scripture set forth for us in the documents of Vatican II. Read the Dogmatic Constitution on the Church. Read the Pastoral Constitution on the Church in the Modern World. There you will find this call for the church to turn itself inside out, to move from self-serving to other-serving. The church is asking all its people to hold themselves responsible for proclaiming the good news to the whole world, and to work to make God's reign come in the whole world.

In summary, then, let me put it like this: The first reason for the existence of the church is to give life. The church has been called to take the place of Jesus in the world. The first business of church, therefore, is to be life giver for all people.

We can put it in a sort of definition form. The church is first and foremost: *community* of God's people, community of *disciples*, called to go out and become for the world a *sign* and a *witness* of Jesus' life-giving presence for "all people that on earth do dwell," and *instrument,* with Jesus and others, for making God's glorious reign come here on earth and in its fullness at the end.

If we are to pass on a life-giving church to our children and our grandchildren, we have to change our way of thinking about church and, even more, our way of living out church. Conversion in thought and action, conversion as individuals and as a parish is the only way the church is going to grow and develop.

What do we adult members of the church need to do to help the church, our parish, change in the way it is supposed to? We are the church. We are the parish. The church, the parish, will not change unless we do something about its conversion.

If we accept this insight into what the church is and what the church is for, if we are open for genuine conversion, then we have some more practical questions to ask. We have some serious homework to do.

The first practical question for all of us is this: Exactly what does it mean to belong to the church, to belong to a parish? How do we work it out?

The question is so simple and so taken for granted that we hardly bother asking it. I am increasingly amazed *(appalled* might be the more appropriate word) at the small percent of churchgoing Catholics who can answer that question in a meaningful way. Most Catholics just don't know what it means to be a member of the church or the parish. In this area we must confess to tremendous ignorance. Our education has been sadly neglected

There is much more to be said. We have to take a look in detail at the radical difference between our present understanding and experience of church, as we have inherited it, and what the church teaches about itself today, particularly through the documents of Vatican II. We have to get a more specific and detailed notion of what it means for us to be "God's people," to be "disciples of the Lord," to be "first-class citizens." We need to know how we can turn this fresh and exciting vision of church into concrete reality through the various ministries that are an essential part of the church's structure. We have to find out how we can take on these ministries, multiply them and make them bear fruit inside and outside the church.

If, after reading this brief summary of what the church is for and what our church is, you want to go further, I recommend that you read the publication *Giving Life: Ministry of the Parish Sunday Assembly.* I have revised it so that it serves as an outline for the entire mission of church in the world today.

2

GOD

The mystery of God cannot be seriously explored among adults until the right beginning is made. The process, once started in the lives of people, makes its own different ways. The Spirit of the Lord, the Spirit of Jesus, always at work, blows where he wills.*

What is it about God that we most importantly need to know, so that we can choose freely and joyfully to be his beloved people? In short, it is this: God, our God, is a life-giving God, a loving God. For us he is nothing else. God loves us, all of us, all people without reservation or exception. God never stops loving us. God loves us when we are in sin just as much as when we are out of sin.

---

*A disclaimer: I often choose to use the masculine pronoun of our biblical ancestors in referring to God in this book. I do this because, frankly, I am not altogether happy with many of the suggested substitutes. Too often they offer over-simplified solutions to a complicated theological issue, and I am not yet ready to settle for them. On the other hand I prefer to avoid the hassle of awkward circumlocutions. I am quite aware that God is spirit and, as unlimited spirit, escapes being impaled on the spit of gender categories. I am aware also that both women and men are made in the image of God. Those who know me are aware of my concern about inclusive language and of my constant effort to avoid sexist terms. I have more to say about this later in this section.

We cannot win God's love. We cannot lose God's love. God is forever faithful. He is the God of covenant love. He has pledged himself forever and he will not go back on his word. His covenant words uttered on Sinai for his chosen people stand firm forever, "I am your God. You are my people. I have chosen you. I choose you. I will save you. I will never let you go."

This is the God of revelation. This is the God of Jesus, the God we must claim. But before we can claim this God we have to look for him and find him. Most of us grew up with an altogether different notion of God. God was way "out" there. The God I got from my catechism and from practically all the preaching that I remember was a distant God, forbidding, often angry, out of reach, unavailable. The person that I thought was God spent most of my young life making me feel guilty. I was a sinner and he was the one who condemned and kept the hell fires burning. Studying philosophy didn't help much, either. There I ran into a god that was fixed point, uncaused cause, immovable mover.

As a consequence of all this brainwashing, I never thought it important to even bother to look for the God of the Bible. I suspect you didn't either. We continued to live with great fear and trepidation of the frightening image of this impersonal and quite unapproachable God that had somehow been drilled into us. At least I did.

Then, thank God, came the deluge. And what a cleansing!

The God of Jesus began to shine through the gray walls — dim at first, not too clear, somewhat uncertain. This God of Jesus began to look more and more like the God I desperately hoped existed somewhere. Jesus' God began to glow with new life: a God of covenant love, a God of unconditional love, a God who loves and loves and loves. This God burst into my world. What a blessing! What a gift! Many of you have experienced, in some way or other, what I am trying to say. If you have, you know what I am babbling about. If you haven't, maybe I can help you a little bit in your own personal discovery.

I remember so well the beginnings of my discovery of what John really meant when he said that God *first* has loved us. God's love is given in his very act of creating us, of bringing us into existence. God's love is pure gift. (It took me a long time to realize what that meant.) God always begins the business of loving us. When we say that God first loved us, we are saying that God always takes the initiative. It means that God's love is never a response to another love. God begins loving and continues loving and never stops loving.

Only God can love *first*. All created people learn to love only when they experience someone else loving them. This is what it means to be a creature. No created person can love *first*. There is no way it can happen. This is what marks the incredible distance between God's love and our love. God does not love at all in the way we do.

Read the parable of the workers in the vineyard. Some work much longer than others but, when they come to get their pay, they all get the same. Big hassle! Lots of grumbling and complaining! God listens courteously and then tells them simply, but so firmly, that it is really none of their business. God loves not in our way but in God's own way. And, wonder of wonders, God cannot love any other way.

To initiate love is to be God; to learn to love is to be a creature. This tremendous insight into God's unique loving power comes clearer when we realize that it is precisely the power to love that God has given us as gift. God has given us the power to love as only God can. In so doing God gives us a share in divine power, a share in divine life. This is the divine gift to all people: God's call to love as he loves and the power to do it. God calls all people to love their brothers and sisters as God does. All people receive the divine power to do so. In this we discover the divine gift and vocation of all God's people.

Two points need pressing in this declaration of God's faithful, unconditional love for all people. First, God's love is for *all* people, not just for those of us who have been chosen as disciples. God does not love Catholics or Christians any more than he loves Jews or Muslims or Hindus or Australian aborigines. As Christians, we have no monopoly on his love, no extra claim. The only extra bonus for us Christians is that we get to *know* about God's love for all people because God has freely chosen to let us know. He has, completely out of generosity, revealed to us Christians the *mystery,* his secret plan to gather all people in Jesus and to bring them back to himself. In the chapter on church I have already noted in more detail how this revelation charges us with the responsibility to proclaim this good news.

People ask often: if God loves everyone and seeks them out anyway, why bother being a Christian? What difference does it make? *Vive la différence!* What a privilege and excitement to know! What a privilege to be called as disciples, to be called into immediate and important partnership with Jesus to help him in his mission! What a privilege to be a sign to brothers and sisters everywhere of God's wonderful, faithful covenant love! People need so desperately to hear that God loves them, to hear about Jesus as a loving brother, a redeeming savior. We are able to tell them. What more do you want?

The second point is that our ever-loving God is a God of power. Our God is also the totally other, the all-holy. But knowing God this way does not, as so many think, remove him from us. Rather, if you look at it the right way, it brings him even closer. This all-powerful God is, like the Bible says, the God who uses his power to support our weakness. This God is not only *with us* but *for us.*

Our ever-loving God is also a God of the impossible. For our God there is no dead end, ever. That means that for us there is no dead end, ever. Our God brings new life and new hope where there is total darkness and total despair. He is always there. The Israelites found this out when God brought them out of hopeless and helpless bondage to new life and new destiny. Out of total, crushing defeat in bloody death, Jesus was raised to new and glorious life. Out of death, new life! Hope against all hope! Faith in total darkness and despair! These are the gifts of our God.

In order to get to know this most amazing and wonderful God, we must destroy a whole pantheon of false gods. You will recognize them, I'm sure. Like me, you worshiped at their shrines at some time or other. If we are honest, we are willing to admit these false gods are hard to shake. They got hold of us when we were young and fastened themselves deep down in the dark places of our unconscious.

God's love is for all people, not just for those of us who have been chosen as disciples. God does not love Catholics or Christians any more than he loves Jews or Muslims or Hindus or Australian aborigines.

First is the legal god, the god who keeps book on you, the god who is just waiting for you to trip up, to snub him, so he can mark you a loser. There are many names for this god: "grim reaper," "policeman in the sky" and so forth. You need to destroy him because he is a false god. "You must not place false gods before me," says the real God.

Other false gods which hold many people in agonized bondage include the god who loves you only when you are good and does not love you when you are bad; the god who will make you pay for all the wrong you have ever done; the god who is expected to fill your empty gas tank so you can make it to the next station and who makes it stop raining so you can have your picnic.

There is also the god who directly causes your misfortunes, the god who withholds salvation from those who do not consciously know of him or who, for whatever misguided reason, deliberately deny his very existence. Not least of all is that god so often invoked by people in power who condemn, persecute, kill and do all kinds of evil in the name of God.

The name of these false gods is Legion. They range all the way from the capricious, unpredictable and malicious gods of the Latin and Greek pantheon to the god who loves you but hates your enemies and will do them in for you. Not least of all is the destructive false god that church people often use to enforce energies destructive of human freedom. These people use God as the "Great Enforcer." They invoke the "will of God" as if they had a direct line to the almighty. It is their easy way of evading responsibility for their own conduct.

Further, it is high time to release God from the bondage of being only a male figure. We have consistently presented God as male for reasons that are easily understandable: Jesus identified God as his Father. Our biblical imagery and church tradition come to us from a male-dominated culture. It is convenient to invoke these reasons to support the limits we arbitrarily place on God. We use the same cultural and traditional excuses for clinging to discrimination patterns against women, in which the church easily participates.

The topic of the *gender* of God is a hot one today, causing anger and alienation — rightly so, because the truth is clear. God defies being limited to a particular and exclusive human sexual identity just as much as she defies being limited to time and space. God is God precisely because he transcends the limits of all that is not God. God manages to escape all the limits we place on her, thank God!

The language and imagery about God is still predominantly masculine. Part of the reason is that we do not know how to handle the matter gracefully. The issue is complex and complicated and allows for no simple solution. We need patience as we explore the possibilities of incorporating feminine imagery into our references to God. Actually, it has already been done a long time ago. No less a person than Isaiah made the astonishing discovery that God was mother as well as father.

Feminine imagery can bring us close to God. We need it. It is not an issue about the *gender* of God. The problem emerges as an inevitable consequence of people's almost complete inability to deal with God as God. In our attempts to understand God we are constantly cutting God down to our size. The process of trying to contain God in human molds never stops. It is like an addiction. The worst state of all is when people work under the delusion that the god they manufacture is the real God.

Linguistically, the problem of sexist language is a problem of pronouns. It seems we need a few more pronouns than we have at the moment.

Right now we need to be open to people who are struggling to go beyond the limitations of masculine language and imagery to express God in an adult and appropriate manner. Christian charity, let alone common courtesy, demands from us every effort to develop as much inclusive language as is possible. Not to do so is to continue to be insensitive to the entire issue of discrimination against women.

The very activity of contemplating the fullness in God of all that we call either male or female can also help males come to terms with their real attitudes toward women, and vice versa.

There is a natural progression in our efforts to get to know and love the real God, the God of unconditional love. First we must be willing to wage relentless warfare on our false gods.

Next we have to find simpler and more familiar imagery for expressing God. In this, we can do no better than to use the imagery close at hand, the imagery we use to express human love and fidelity and friendship in its various forms. It all fits. Rosemary Haughton, a British housewife and theologian, for instance, speaks of God as our "passionate lover." It is true, because that is precisely the kind of lover God is. Getting used to this kind of language is not an easy task because people generally have become numbed by all the "God-talk" they have heard and still hear. The language of the prayers at Mass doesn't help at all. I doubt these prayers say anything important to people.

In this process of getting to know God there are clearly marked stages: first, you get the idea that somehow God loves all people without exception. After you get used to that remarkable insight, you begin to grasp the realization that God loves *us.* Finally, you begin to grapple with the stunning truth: *God loves me! Wow!*

As we struggle to accept this God of love, we are more and more able to free ourselves from the grisly grip of our false gods. It's like this: any effort we make to get rid of our false gods frees us up to find the real God of love. At the same time our efforts to discover the real God of love helps us do battle against our false gods.

For this cleansing process I recommend strong doses of the Bible. I recommend that you get all the fine materials that are available today to help you understand the Bible: there are books and tapes and periodicals galore. For starters, read Ephesians. Look for the themes of God's unique love that occur regularly in the Sunday scripture readings: the prodigal father, the woman taken in adultery, the good shepherd and many more. Once you start looking for this theme you will be amazed at how quickly you find what you are searching for.

As we go along we learn that there are all kinds of gods in the Bible. At first this is disturbing. Will the real God please stand up? What we have to know is that many of them are not the real God. These gods represent the limited understanding of God that obtained in the time, culture and understanding of those who wrote the passages. We learn gradually to submit all these past and present images of God to the God of love that Jesus revealed.

As we find these false gods wanting, we destroy them deliberately and ruthlessly.

It is just too bad that so much of our Sunday preaching does not help very much. Preachers have to go through the same process that we are talking about. Some do. Many do not. When you find those who try, encourage them. They can use your help.

The heartwarming part of all this is that we don't have to do it all by ourselves. As we make our efforts to reach out to the *real* God, she is already there reaching out to help us. In fact, God is reaching out to us long before we even start reaching out to him. God gives us the sight to see, the heart to be sure and the faith to surrender. God is always saying to us, to you, to me: "I am here. I am with you. I am for you. I love you."

Jesus is the only real starting point for understanding the God who is with us and for us. Jesus is the visible image of the invisible God. Jesus is the only one who has claimed to know the Father and to reveal the Father to us. He has made it quite clear that no one comes to God except through him, that no one knows God except through his revelation.

When we start with Jesus as God's way to us and our way to God, we start with the simple fact that we cannot know God directly. So we don't try. We accept that fact and live with it comfortably. God comes to us through us. Long ago, Romano Guardini said it: "Man is God's way to man." (I am sure that today he would hasten to say: "People are God's way to people," or something like it.)

God becomes available to all people through the experiences that people share with one another. This is the regular and ordinary way in which God reveals self to us. In fact, God doesn't do it any other way. God has chosen to become available in human form: first through Israel, then through Jesus and now through us.

The pattern is always the same: first, there is an experience, then the awareness that there is more to the experience than we see or hear or feel. Then comes the moment of recognition, the cry of sure knowledge: God is here! God is present! God is touching me! (All this happens, of course, through the power of the Spirit: pure gift!)

Take Israel's exodus experience for an instance. First, the experience: a band of slaves was brought to freedom by their leader, Moses. After the event came the sharing of the experience, the recounting of the experience, the anniversaries. Precisely in and through the sharing and remembering dawns the growing awareness, the certainty, that it was not Moses who saved them. Moses was an instrument. God was the one who really freed them. God is the one who is continuing to make them more free. God is the one who is calling them to a freedom they only dimly perceive. All this takes place, of course, at the initiative of and under the direction of the Spirit of God.

Linguistically, the problem of sexist language is a problem of pronouns. It seems we need a few more pronouns than we have at the moment.

Through oral tradition, the story grows: anniversaries become more and more revealing. The people become more and more sure and certain in their remembering and praising and thanking. Finally the full-blown story gets written down in the Book of Exodus. The physical experience of gaining freedom from Egyptian oppression is gradually transformed, under the revealing power of God's Spirit, into the universal exodus story.

And with Israel's exodus story comes the startling insight that God is first revealed to the chosen people as *liberator,* as the one who frees us from bondage and leads us on to freedom. The punishing god, the avenging god, the warrior god all came later. None of them measure up to the God who makes us free.

This is a sample of how God comes to us. The same pattern can be traced in the life of Jesus. The disciples got to know God through daily contact with Jesus. We can make the same contact ourselves, through each other, through the scriptures and through all kinds of simple human experiences.

I happen to be writing this book at the ocean. Each morning I go out on the beach. Again and again I find myself caught in the experience of something that is "more" than what is there. The presence of God touches me through the majesty and power of ocean and shore. I do not touch God; God touches me. I have nothing to do with the experience except to be open to it, to receive it, to taste it, to embrace it, and to respond with wonder and joy and thanks and gladness. God comes because God is already there. All I can do about it is be open to God's being there.

I repeat: all we can do about God's coming into our lives is to be open. The more we are open to each other, the more we are making ourselves open to God.

There is one time and place in which we really can help each other discover God. It is Sunday Mass. One of the most important reasons why people go to Mass on Sunday is to have some contact with God. More times than not they are denied this contact because of the dull and lifeless patterns of Sunday Mass. It takes a great deal of understanding and a lot of homework to make Sunday Mass the experience of God that it can and should be.

We can all help Sunday Mass become a good experience of God. The parish Sunday assembly must release three major energies in order to make a life-giving celebration. They must gather. They must listen. They must respond through eucharist and through mission.

We can do a lot about making these three energies come alive. For instance, people who come to Mass in Catholic churches are not particularly inclined to pay much attention to each other. They are inclined to be closed in on themselves, each lost in a world of individual piety. Hospitality is not exactly the hallmark of Catholic Sunday Mass. All you have to do is to start paying attention to other people. Come early and talk with them.

Get to know more people. Get other people to do the same. When you help people to be open to each other, you are leading them in a sure way of getting to touch God and God to touch them.

The liturgy of the word should be a *listening* experience for all people at Mass. In most parishes it is not. The liturgy of the word can and should be a contemplative experience. All the ingredients are at hand. All we need to know is how to put them together.

We must rid ourselves of the notion that the contemplative experience is the esoteric exception, reserved only for the few. The contemplative moment is well within the range of all people; it can be easy to come by, if the obstacles are removed.

One of the simplest ways to help people gain their own experience of God is to help design the service of the word, in whatever way you can, so that this contemplative experience can happen. The ingredients are clear and manageable: reading, listening, silence, personal response, communal response. Get readers who read — and *mean* — the word. Listen with all the energy you can. Savor and reflect in silence and then respond in word and song. Instead of talking in hushed, mysterious, meaningless words about the *transcendent* God, help people discover for themselves that God is there. Instead of trying to find God in dim light and candles and incense, help people to find God where he most is: in other people, even at Mass. Help them do whatever is necessary for them to be open and receptive. The rest is up to God, and God is faithful.

Get involved as much as you can in the response. Listen to the story of the eucharistic prayer and make it your own. Don't just stand on the edges of it and figure you have heard it all many times before. Each time can be an experience, if you take the trouble to get involved. Do it. Encourage others to do it. See what a difference it makes in your growing encounter with God!

Finally, go out from Mass making a point of touching the lives of other people with some kind of care and generosity. We can hardly measure how much happens to us through these encounters. We all have enough experiences about giving life to others. We all know just how much it means when we touch them and let them touch us. There is no limit. It is in these experiences of personal encounter that, perhaps most of all, we touch God and God touches us.

If you want more detail about this process at Sunday Mass, I refer you to other publications of mine such as *Giving Life: Ministry of the Parish Sunday Assembly* (Assembly Edition; Leader's Guide); *Celebration: Theology, Ministry and Practice; Proclaiming God's Love in Word and Deed;* and *Proclaiming God's Love in Song.*

God is the focus of countless tomes and treatises. I have dared to speak of God in a single chapter. But I do believe that these few notions about God, so disarmingly simple, are the right beginning for helping adults get in touch with an adult God.

The mystery of God just cannot be seriously explored among adults until the right beginning is made. Once the process is started in the lives of people, it makes its own different ways. The Spirit of the Lord, the Spirit of Jesus, always at work, blows where he wills. Our task, as responsible adults, is to point the way, to clear away the massive obstacles encrusted upon our culture and to help people get started.

This is precisely the task of responsible adults. Adults are responsible for each other. Adults are called, before all else, to be lovers and life givers, just like God. Just like Jesus. The miracle is that, when we take the trouble to break down the barriers that separate us from other people, we necessarily break through to God because that is exactly where God is. Don't worry about touching God so much. Take the trouble to touch your neighbor and God will touch you.

3
JESUS

Who is Jesus? What is he for? What is his relationship with God and with the church and with people? Is Jesus for real? How do we get in touch with him? In asking these questions I am trying to put my finger on how Jesus knew and understood himself and how we can know and understand Jesus. Jesus' whole life was lived out in relationship to God, to the arrival of God's reign and to people, particularly his disciples. We can get to know Jesus only in and through these different relationships.

Jesus, for himself, was never an end unto himself. Jesus, for us, should never be seen or understood as an end in himself, because he is not. Jesus is *the way*. Jesus is God's way to us and our way to God. If we really hold onto this idea and really learn its meaning, we can get to know Jesus as far as it is at all possible.

If we lose the idea of Jesus as *the way*, we shall fall into the classical errors about Jesus: we shall exalt him as Lord so high that he goes out of reach, or we shall so humanize him that we lose him as God. Jesus is mystery, just like God, or church, or the human person. He will always escape our attempts to catch him and put him into any given category. The litmus test is simple: once we think we have Jesus figured out, we can be sure that he has escaped and that our search must begin again.

An important step in the process of adults getting to know Jesus is to take away the pedestal where most of us try to keep him. Catholic adults readily know that Jesus is God and that Jesus is the Son of God. They do not seem to grasp nearly as well an equally important truth about Jesus: that he is indeed our brother.

Jesus is one of us. He belongs to us and we belong to him because we both belong to the same human family. Jesus is our friend and brother in every sense of the word. We can identify with Jesus because he has forever identified himself with us.

The problem for most all Catholic adults lies precisely in getting to know Jesus as friend and brother, and relating to Jesus as friend and brother. We usually do not have any trouble with the God part, but we can't seem to hold onto the human part well. How can we learn to accept Jesus as brother and live comfortably with him as brother? How can we live with Jesus as friend? What can I do in this short chapter to help you in your efforts to get to know Jesus better as friend and brother? I am not sure what I can do but I am going to try.

The best I can do is to speak from my own experience. I can tell you how I came to "discover" Jesus, and how I go about helping other people to "discover Jesus. I can talk only about my own personal experience. Maybe what I say can help you to get in touch with your own experience. Maybe I can make some beginning suggestions about how to find Jesus, who is indeed the Lord but who is with us and like us in all things except sin.

Jesus is with us. Jesus is available. This is the first good news that makes an exciting and thrilling difference in the lives of grownups. He is not dead and gone, a figure of history only. We don't need to reach back into a shadowy and vague past to find Jesus. He is not there. He is right here.

"Jesus is risen and he is with us!" This is the heart of the Christian proclamation from the beginning. "Now hear this! Now hear this! Jesus is risen and he is *with* us!" When this familiar proclamation begins to become more than mere nice words we begin, under the power of the Spirit, to really believe that Jesus is for real and that we can get in touch with him. In a real sense

Jesus is closer to us today than he ever was even to his own disciples before his death and resurrection. I would like to help you understand what I mean by that statement.

The first thing I would like to do is tell the story of Jesus. It all starts with the Father talking to his Son: "Go to my people. Become one of them. Identify with them, live among them and be one of them. Tell them how much I love them. Better yet, show them how much I love them. Give yourself to them and for them.

"Talk to them about my plans for them. Tell them how I want them to live with me forever. Let them know that you are going to make your way back to me and that you will show them the same way back to me, and that you will help them on the way back.

"Gather them together and make disciples of those whom you choose and who will accept you. Gradually teach them by word and example that your way is not a way of power and might, but a way of suffering and dying and rising to new life. It is going to be mighty hard for you. There will be times when you will want to quit. Try to remember, when things get difficult, that I am with you and I will not let you down."

Now listen to Jesus talking to his disciples and to us. "I am going away for a while. After I am put to death and raised up you will no longer be able to see me or touch me in my physical body. Nor will anyone else be able to reach me through my physical body.

"So when I am gone, you must go to my people. You must be me. It is through you that I mean to be present to my people and to continue my saving work among them. You must become my living body in a world of living bodies. You must identify with my people just as I did. You show them and tell them how much I love them, how much my father loves them. You reach out and touch them with love and compassion and care and healing. I will be with you all the time. Through all the efforts that you make to give them something of yourself, I will enter their lives and become life giver and friend and brother to them all.

"You have the power to hold me captive or to release me and my saving love into the lives of other people. It is up to you to break down the barriers. It is up to you to open the doors so that I can get through. This is your task and your business. I need you to do it. I depend on you to do it."

It all starts with the Father talking to his Son: "Go to my people. Become one of them. Identify with them, live among them and be one of them. Tell them how much I love them. Better yet, show them how much I love them. Give yourself to them and for them."

Jesus did what God told him. He came; he identified and spoke about God's love. More importantly he showed what God's love was all about by the way he loved others. He preached the reign of God and he gathered his disciples. He lived, he suffered, he died, he was raised up and he went back to his father. However, that's not the end of the story. He did not leave his first followers in a despairing, miserable huddle in the upper room.

Jesus came back! He was raised up and, through the power of the mighty Spirit of God which now became his own Spirit, he exploded into the presence of his followers. He gave them the power to *see* him, to *know* him, to *believe* in him. The resurrection stories of the gospel tell us some of the many ways that Jesus made believers and disciples of them for the rest of their lives.

After the resurrection of Jesus, the disciples experienced the real breakthrough. Up to this time, they were not sure of anything, really. During their time with Jesus they had glimpses, faint ones, of the divinity of Christ. These glimpses apparently disappeared, however, as fast as they came. Look at the disciples gathered in the upper room after Jesus died and was buried. You certainly do not see a picture of strong believers.

Then came the resurrection. Then came their own personal

experience of the risen Jesus! What a change! What a breakthrough! That's when they really got the picture, strong, sharp, clear. No mistake now. No doubts. No fear. No wonder they acted as if they were drunk! "Jesus, our master, our rabbi, our teacher, our friend and brother, is the Lord God!"

This event and realization was enough to send this tiny band of people on the biggest "trip" the world has ever known. It is because of that trip that we are here today talking about Jesus. We ourselves are now about the task of becoming disciples and believers and, like our predecessors, we are helping to make believers and disciples out of those who are our own people.

The important question for us is: How did Jesus, when he was on earth, get his disciples to love him so much, to feel so close to him, so loyal to him, so committed to him? How did he get to love them so much? The answer to this question is important for us because the way Jesus did it then is exactly the way he does it now. He did it then through simple human signs, signs that he made through his own body. He does it now through signs he makes, not through his own body, but through us, through our bodies. Let me explain further.

When Jesus was on earth, he got to know his friends and neighbors in the same way that we do. He lived with them, he touched them, he spent time with them. He laughed with them and he cried with them. He went to their weddings and funerals. Jesus made friends with John and Peter just the way we make friends. There was no magic at all; they got to know him, love him and become attached to him because of his personal attractiveness.

Jesus attracted different people in different ways, just as we do. Jesus had different kinds of relationships with his disciples due to his own temperament and their different personalities. John speaks often of his love for Jesus. John's relationship with Jesus was quite different from Peter's. It is plain that Peter and Jesus, two different kinds of men, developed a strong and deep relationship. The disciples, by the power of the Spirit, gained faith because of their human experiences with Jesus.

It is precisely because we are living bodies that Jesus comes to us through us. Everything was fine for the disciples until Jesus died and was raised up. Then they could no longer see him or touch him. People with bodies have to see and touch, and be seen and touched. It is the only way they can communicate with anyone. So Jesus did a simple but remarkable thing. He made his disciples and all people in the whole world his body. Jesus deliberately chose to use the human signs that people make as his way to be present to us, to relate to us and to let us relate to him.

Jesus is alive and present in the whole world; he is risen and is glorified. This means that he is not bound by the limits of time or the limits of space. He is present and active everywhere. Despite the images we have received from the past, Jesus is not seated somewhere on a throne at the right side of his Father holding the Spirit between them. Jesus is active. Jesus is laboring among us. He is still doing the task he came to do.

"I am always with you." Is this just nice rhetoric, or do we really believe it? Jesus will not stop working until the job is done, and that will be at the end of time, whatever that means. Jesus continues to be busy giving to all people his new life, his life of freedom and joy. Jesus works through *us* to give this new life to us, to those whom we touch.

This is important. We, *all people*, have the power to give Jesus' life to one another, or to deny that life to one another. Whenever people anywhere pay attention to other people, care for them, help them, are open to them in any way, they give the new risen life of Jesus. There is no other life for people. Through Jesus, through us, in the power of the Spirit, God gives his life and saving love to all people. What I am saying is real gospel, not just nice theories to make people feel good.

Take a breather from my efforts to explain, and pick up the

Gospel of Matthew, the end of chapter 25. Read carefully the words of Jesus about final judgment and the heavenly reign. Read his words about how our lives will be measured in terms of the kind of attention we give to other people.

Those who are listening to Jesus in the parable don't know what to make of his words. "Lord, we never saw you hungry or thirsty or in prison. We never gave you food or drink, or got you out of jail." But he tells them that they have done it for him any time they have done it for anybody else anywhere. That's it. Anyone to anyone anywhere. You don't have to know Jesus or have any intention of doing anything for him or in his name. All you have to do is turn in love and mercy and thoughtfulness to a brother or sister. In your turning you meet Jesus and Jesus meets you. You may not recognize him all the time, but that is what happens.

We do not give any more of Jesus' life to brothers and sisters than anyone else simply because we are Catholic or Christian. The only difference is that we can know what we are doing and we can do it deliberately. Jesus has revealed his intentions to us, his father's plan and how he means to carry it out. This revelation is our privilege, and we rejoice in it. But it is also our responsibility to proclaim and share this revelation. That's what disciples are all about. That is what the business of "evangelization" is all about.

It is up to us, however it becomes possible, to proclaim the good news. That is truly an intoxicating ministry: to be able to proclaim to the whole world that Jesus is alive and active in our world, in all people, making himself friend and brother to all people through all people.

When grown-up men and women get to know how close they can get to Jesus and how much they can help Jesus get close to others, they get excited. They begin to see a whole new world of life and hope. They get a new sense of direction. There's important work to be done. People begin to get a whole new sense of meaning to life. Their vision grows beyond the narrow confines of their own tight little world. Many find a sense of mission and want to do something about it. They want to tell others.

Let's explore further what it means to say that Jesus is like us in all things except sin. It means that Jesus knows and appreciates friendship, good humor, good food and drink. It means that Jesus really did enjoy parties. Jesus did laugh and sing and dance. Can you imagine Jesus, at the Cana wedding, sitting back in the corner with mama while all his friends were out there dancing? If you can imagine this, you haven't caught onto the real Jesus yet.

It means that Jesus knows fear and anger, uncertainty and loneliness. Jesus knows real temptation. He knows what it is like to be misunderstood, cut off, betrayed. He knows what it is like to be in the desperate blackness of not knowing for sure whether God cares for him or not. Yes, Jesus knows it all because he has experienced it all. Jesus has been there. What a blessing to discover this Jesus! What a blessing and a mighty joy!

Infallible figures on thrones are remote: we can admire them from a distance but we cannot identify with them. Genuine empathy is not possible. We stay where we are, and they stay where they are. We can be "interested" in Caesar, George Washington, other figures of history or our saints and heroes. They, too, were human, but they are gone away. Only the memory remains, and that tends to fade fast.

The discovery that Jesus is not a far-off memory but really alive makes a tremendous difference. It changes the whole picture. Jesus is Lord, the Son of God, to be sure, but also a fully human person. That is the side of Jesus that is being rediscovered today. We need to become familiar with it because we get to the God side through the human side.

Jesus is a mystery, a mystery deep as God, a mystery beyond our full comprehension. But we fall short if we simply acknowledge the mystery of Jesus and then put Jesus back on some distant throne. Adults today are well able to hear what the theologians and scripture scholars are telling us about Jesus. They can indeed understand what Bruce Vawter was saying in his book, *This Man Jesus,* what Raymond Brown was saying in *The Birth of the Messiah* and what Gerard Sloyan was saying in *Jesus in Focus.*

Take a breather from my efforts to explain, and pick up the Gospel of Matthew, the end of chapter 25. Read carefully the words of Jesus about final judgment and the heavenly reign. Read his words about how our lives will be measured in terms of the kind of attention we give to other people.

Not only *can* today's adults deal with this scholarship, they *need* to discover more about Jesus as a human being. The need is great. For many, it is a matter either of developing a lively faith in Jesus or of closing him off and walking away. What most adult Catholics learned as children about Jesus is meager nourishment for them. If they do not get more, they starve or remain children.

Adults really need to know that nothing in the life of Jesus was phony. Too many people assume that Jesus had it made, no matter what, and that he *knew* all along that he had it made. In this primitive notion, Jesus always had a mental image of himself as being God. If that image were true, Jesus as a human was not for real at all. If it were true, we would be right in concluding that Jesus played a game, that he tricked us.

Thankfully, game-playing is not what Jesus is about. Every single experience he had, whether joy or pain or sorrow or desolation, was real. This is basically what the scripture scholars and theologians are saying about Jesus. On that they agree, regardless of the refined differences among their various theories.

The incarnation, life, death and resurrection of Jesus took place under the power and direction of the Spirit of God. The Spirit of God presided over and guided all that took place in the life of Jesus, just as the same Spirit presided over all that God has done in the affairs of people from the beginning of creation. In all the experiences of his life, and in all the relationships of his life, Jesus was drawn to his destiny under the power of the Spirit.

Through these experiences Jesus learned who he was, what his work was to be. Gradually, he became aware of the unique relationship he had with God. Under the power of the Spirit he was led to recognize and acknowledge that relationship as Father-Son — not just any father-son relationship, but a unique one.

Jesus became aware that his task was to preach God's glorious reign. More importantly, Jesus came to know that the God's reign was coming through himself. Jesus started off as a disciple of John the Baptizer, whom he had chosen to follow. Only after John was killed did Jesus seem to get the whole picture. As the clouds of anger and hatred began to gather and cling to him, Jesus became more and more aware that he was destined to bring about God's reign not only through preaching, but through suffering and death. By the power of the Spirit he was led to say a complete and total "Yes." No one really knows when that moment finally and completely happened. Some will say that the fullness of his being and destiny burst on him at the moment of his last cry at the cross.

Certainly his agony in the garden was real. He was terrified. In his whole being, he recoiled. He did not want to go on. Most terrible of all was his sense of having been abandoned by the one person who was always with him, his God, whom he called Father. He was cut off. There was no consoling hand to touch him, no tender word to encourage him. He was alone. Still, with power of which he was probably unaware, he held fast. He was committed in his whole being to do what he was sent to do, to bring about the coming of God's reign.

No matter what pain or separation or desolation we ourselves can ever experience, we can know that Jesus has truly been there himself. That is why we can identify with him. He is there all the time, even when we neither know nor feel his presence. He is here with us in the way God was there with him.

Rediscover the Jesus of the gospel. Make the story of Jesus brand new again for yourself. Accept him as friend and brother. Begin to deal with him as you would deal with a friend. Talk with him in your own familiar way. Be comfortable with him. Enjoy his presence and share him with others. Find other people to explore with you this most wonderful person whose name is Jesus.

4
SPIRIT

Before we talk about the Spirit, let's make sure that we are ready to do it right. Let's make sure we don't cut God up into three parts and then cut one part off from the others. Most people know only one formula for naming the Trinity: "In the name of the Father *and* of the Son *and* of the Holy Spirit."

I call this the *separation* formula. This formula persuades us to think of three distinct and separate persons, each about his own business, without too much reference to the others. It does not deny the other side of the Trinity, that God is one and indivisible, but tends to play it down. This separation formula makes it easy for us to set up three shrines, putting the Father in one, Jesus in another and the Spirit in the last one. Then we tend to close the doors on these neat shrines and go about our special and separate cults and devotions. And we wonder why another person does not share our enthusiasm for our own particular cult.

We need to reclaim the original, dynamic formula for expressing the Trinity. This is the formula recommended for closing the first public prayer at Mass, the prayer of the faithful, but it is not being used much. Maybe we have gotten so used to it that it doesn't mean much to us. The standard formula goes like this: "Grant this through our Lord Jesus Christ, your Son, who lives and reigns with you and the Holy Spirit, one God, for ever and ever." Maybe the language is too formal. It could go like this: "We pray this through our Lord Jesus Christ, your son and our brother, who lives and works with you and with us in the power of the

Holy Spirit." The language is more in the style in which we talk with each other.

The formula is dynamic. It suggests relationship. It is filled with images of action, change, power, energy: "To the Father through Jesus in the power of the Spirit." The other way round: "From the Father through Jesus in the power of the Spirit." This formula attempts to hold the mystery of unity and dynamic relation all mixed up into one. That is exactly what the *mystery* of God is all about: Father, Son and Spirit can never be taken apart. As soon as you get any one of these carefully captured and think you understand clearly, you have lost the whole mystery and need to start all over again.

We pray this through our Lord Jesus Christ, your son and our brother, who lives and works with you and with us in the power of the Holy Spirit.

In my time the Spirit got a passing nod at Pentecost and at confirmations. Confirmation texts spoke of the coming of the Spirit as if he hadn't been around since birth and baptism. Apart from these special occasions we did not hear much or read much about the activity of the Spirit. Occasionally banner makers would offer their various versions of doves to represent the Spirit. They meant well, and the bird image is certainly part of our tradition, but they actually succeeded in putting the Spirit out of bounds. I, for one, do not relate too well to a bird.

Some people are declaring the present decades to be particularly a time and season of the Spirit. It is as if the Father had his time, retired, and turned over the action to Jesus. Then Jesus retired and turned over the action to the Spirit. It all sounds pretty ridiculous to me.

We don't chop God up that way. We don't divide God's creative energy into different human historical times and then assign particular times to particular persons of the Trinity. We must avoid the well-intentioned, three-act salvation history play in which God leads off, then yields front stage to Jesus, then both sit down and let the Spirit to do the remainder of the drama. This kind of imagery is foolishness. It must be avoided. The first truth that we know for sure about the Trinity is that *we don't know.* After that, we try as best we can to understand the Trinity as it has been revealed to us.

The startling surge of the charismatic movement has brought the Spirit to a level of attention not experienced in the church, at least in our time. For all its valuable contribution, this charismatic emphasis on the Spirit tends to create some difficulties. There is a tendency to capture the Spirit, to separate him from the Father and the Son and to hold him apart. I certainly am not indicting the basic value of the charismatic renewal; I am merely describing what I think is an observable tendency to divide the Trinity in a way that can lead up blind alleys and bring people to dead ends.

For all these reasons I think there are some clear revelations about the Spirit of God that all adults should know and understand. I would like to state briefly what they are.

Whenever we speak of the Spirit of God we are necessarily speaking about all the life-giving energy of God that has ever touched the world or ever will.

In biblical revelation the term "Spirit of God" is used to represent the fullness of the creative energy of God. It has been so from the beginning. The Spirit of God is represented as brooding over primordial chaos. This Spirit brought forth the full magnificence of all creation. The same Spirit continues to work God's marvelous deeds among people. God's creative act was not a once-and-for-all act after which God went back and sat down. The same fullness of God's creative Spirit that brought creation out of nothing is needed to "keep it going." So the Spirit continues to energize all creation and all life therein. The Spirit of the Lord fills the earth. Nothing is outside the creative work of the

Spirit. Without the power of the Spirit of God, nothing and no one exists and achieves fullness of being .

Even though the Spirit of God is at work everywhere and is always sustaining life and bringing all creation to its final destiny in God's reign, there are some special events in which we are able to catch startling insights into the work of God among people.

The one outstanding event that brings to focus the work of God's Spirit is the event that we call Jesus. The Spirit of God presided over the conception and birth of Jesus. The Spirit of God, as we have already pointed out at some length, brought Jesus along the way of his whole life. The Spirit led Jesus to full awareness of himself and his task. Through the power of the Spirit of God, Jesus was able to bring to a shattering conclusion his mission on earth. Through the power of the Spirit Jesus gave himself over to death and was raised to his new life of glory. Through the power of the Spirit Jesus won his victory and leaped forever from the bondage of unredeemed human life to the freedom of the total life of God. Through the power of the Spirit of God, Jesus made his exodus back to the Father and reached the fullness of God's life.

Because Jesus cooperated so completely with the Spirit of God leading him to his destiny, he was given full possession of the Spirit of God as his own Spirit. Through the resurrection the Spirit of God became forever the Spirit of Jesus. Jesus was empowered to send his own Spirit, the Spirit of God, into the world to bring all people, whether they know it or not, to their final destiny in the heavenly reign.

As we get to realize this amazing and wonderful truth about the Spirit we enter more deeply into the mystery of God. Our insights are not total and complete. Only God knows God the way God really is. Our insights are enough, however, to help us to touch God and to help us know how God touches us. It is enough that God has touched us through Jesus in the power of the Spirit. One Father, one Jesus, one Spirit — all in one God.

There are two further understandings which adults must have in order to enter more fully into the life-giving work and energy of the Spirit.

First, we need to know that the presence and power of the Spirit is always active on our behalf. The energy of God is always set at full speed ahead. God is *with* us and *for* us all the time. Where God is — and that is everywhere — life is changed, hope is possible and exile is ended.

Only one thing can frustrate or stop the work of the Spirit: having a closed mind and heart. Nothing else. The Spirit is pure gift. The only requirement is to be open enough to receive the gift. We don't have to know about it. We don't even have to know that there is a Spirit working in us and for us. The only requirement is not to be closed.

God is constantly seeking us to be covenant partners, to turn to him and be converted to him. God is doing this through the Spirit of Jesus. The Spirit of Jesus is alive and active in our world and in our lives. Jesus is constantly seeking us out, calling us to pay attention to him by paying attention to one another. God seeks us out and comes into our lives through the Spirit of Jesus. Say it almost any way you want. Emphasize the Father, the Son or the Spirit, it really does not make much difference. The truth, however expressed, is that God is always present and at work in our lives.

Second, we need to realize that the Spirit of Jesus is present and available to *all* people equally. The Spirit is not given to some and refused to others. No one can lay any claim of privilege: the Spirit of Jesus is leading all people back to God and to their destiny in the heavenly reign. Whether they know it or not, all people are under the power and influence of the Spirit. The Spirit always knows. The Spirit always cares. We can depend on the Spirit just as Jesus did.

Only one thing can frustrate or stop the work of the Spirit: having a closed mind and heart. Nothing else. The Spirit is pure gift. The only requirement is to be open enough to receive the gift. We don't have to know about it. We don't even have to know that there is a Spirit working in us and for us. The only requirement is not to be closed.

What is more, all of us have a sure sign by which we can determine whether we are open or closed. It is a sure test. If we are open to other people, we are open to the Spirit. If we are closed to other people, we are closed to the Spirit.

In the church the Spirit is relentlessly at work bringing the church to an awareness of its destiny and its mission, raising up people inside the church and outside the church to lead it on its way. As church, we make mistakes, become confused and do bad things. We get some good leaders and some bad leaders. History is clear on that.

Despite the mess we make, the Spirit still pulls us on. A static concept of the Spirit, combined with a reluctance to acknowledge the humanity of Jesus, causes some church members to presume, sometimes rather arrogantly, that the church and church leaders can do no wrong or that the church does all things right. Children of all ages buy that. Adults do not, because they know it isn't true.

Our more sound and healthy understanding of the Spirit helps us see that God cares very much for a human and sinful church and will not abandon it. This understanding bears with it a great reverence for the mystery that is the Spirit of God. It helps us avoid being so cocksure that God is always on our side. It leads us to a humble belief and hope that the Spirit of the Lord is always there, offering light to all who are truly open. It leads us to search for a forgiving spirit when some church leaders pull their power plays.

A last word: The Spirit moves where the Spirit wills. If we

are open, we will discover the Spirit in all kinds of unexpected places. Unfortunately, too many people tend to think that the Spirit comes full force only on those special occasions when we pray, "Come, Spirit." As a result, they miss most of the movement of the Spirit. Adults know the Spirit comes through all the experiences we have in our encounters with the created universe, from sunsets to the deepest moments of love. No respecter of persons or office, the Spirit speaks with equal force through the church community, through Gandhi or Dorothy Day, through a Cambodian peasant or a prophetic "secular" author or the mother of a family. We can discern only to a degree through whom or in what way the Spirit speaks most authentically.

People who keep themselves conscious of this utter freedom of the Spirit of God tend to keep themselves more ready for the Spirit than others. They are, in a sense, wide open and more apt to sense the Spirit's energy and to cooperate in the Spirit's work, whenever or wherever the Spirit's presence is felt.

5
CHRISTIAN FAITH

It is a pity to see grown-up men and women in bondage to childish, even harmful notions about faith. It used to be fashionable to say that the "faith of an untutored Breton peasant" was quite good enough for any person. This is pious nonsense. Another shibboleth of equal foolishness is the word that has been handed down from above for many decades: "Don't disturb the faith of the people." Both of these notions have been generated, it seems, out of the mindset I would call clerical paternalism. Centuries of clerical paternalism seem almost like a conspiracy to keep adults from becoming real grownups.

These concepts are at home in what I call the "playground" image of church. This "playground" church has barbed wire fences and high walls with broken glass on top. There are lots of "security" guards. In this "secure" playground all adults who are under authority are expected to stay put and obey the rules. "Don't ask grown-up questions. Don't engage in speculation about the things you are ask to believe in. Don't try to break bounds. We will take good care of you. Just do as you are told. Daddy knows best."

This model has many roots. It derives, most of all, from the distorted notion of authority and blind obedience that has for so long prevailed in the church. It is also fed by various and sundry distortions of the Good Shepherd image. Instead of focusing on the admirable characteristics of care and devotion typical of the shepherd, it tends to assume that church members are like a flock of bleating, follow-the-leader sheep. A more grim image of this notion is found in the chapter, "The Grand Inquisitor," in the Dostoievsky novel *The Brothers Karamazov.* Another classic expression of the same model is the bondage of the captives in Plato's allegory of the cave.

The time of this bondage is over. It can no longer prevail. There has been a revolution among adults everywhere who will no longer be treated like children. In assistance of this revolution, Vatican II has issued a strong call that all adults take up and claim again their rightful status as grownups and as first-class citizens in the church. The response to this call is becoming quite vocal. The natives are restless.

All this is preliminary to what we want to say about Christian faith. At the popular level this word "faith" has many meanings. For this reason it is difficult to use the word without generating some confusion. The word "faith" is used often to describe a body of revealed truths that Catholic people are expected to believe in. More commonly it is used to name the reasoned and intellectual assent that people give to the propositions of this revealed truth. This kind of faith assent finds expression in the various creedal formulas that we recite at baptisms and at Sunday Mass.

Faith, in its deepest meaning, is none of the above. Faith is, before anything else, an *experience.* It is the experience of the encounter of one living person with another living person. At the religious level faith is the name of a living relationship we have with God through Jesus in the power of the Spirit. Only adults can make a full faith response. Only an adult can choose to relate to another person. Only adults can enter fully and deliberately into the relationship that we call faith.

For this reason the faith of a child, or of a childlike person, is hopelessly inadequate for an adult, whether sophisticated or not, whether educated or not. The faith of a grown-up person must be able to live and grow comfortably with all the tough questions and doubts that are the normal predicament of any person growing from childhood through adolescence to healthy, responsible adult life.

In this chapter we aim to explore what it means to exchange a childhood kind of faith for a genuine adult faith response. How do children of all ages get from childhood faith to adult faith?

In this process the first order of business will be to "disturb the faith of our people." I am guilty, because I am going to do it deliberately. If we do not do some disturbing there will be no ongoing conversion. Lack of ongoing conversion will cause much disturbance later in life.

When children begin to change into adults, the faith they think they have is likely to shrivel up and disappear or harden into a defensive closed-off caricature of what an adult's faith should be. What they learned as children about God and Jesus and all the rest of church teaching is not adequate for an adult life. A child can take in just so much. It is interesting that the most important area of life in which people tend not to grow up is the area of faith.

It is sad to see grown-up men and women cling to what they learned as children and think that what they know is all there is to know. They are fearful of change: they feel that attempts to enlarge their world of faith are plots and attacks by those who have no faith. This is a pitiful state for grown-up people. It should be recognized as pitiable and not smilingly glorified as something sweet and lovely. Let's do "disturb the faith of our people" and help them throw out all the childish and adolescent faith baggage they continue to drag around.

There are two different ways of "disturbing" the faith of people. One way is reckless, disrespectful and pastorally insensitive to their needs, their fears, their pains. To act this way toward people is itself most childish. There is another way, one that is healthy, responsible and supportive. That is the one we want to talk about here.

I would like to set before you just the bare bones of the kind of knowledge and attitudes about faith that adults need if they are to live rich and fruitful lives. My presumption is that a lot of people *do* want to grow up. There are enough responsible people around who are willing to plot with each other to escape from the "playground."

Freedom becomes desirable and possible when grownups begin to understand what adult faith is all about. In order to uncover this proper understanding we have to break through a lot of superficial jargon about faith. We have to puncture popular clichés and debunk a number of myths.

One of the clichés is the expression that faith is a "gift." It is easy enough to say. I am not so sure, however, that we really know what it means. The word comes too easily and just as quickly passes away. I suspect that the word "gift" leaves most people with a "thing" image. Gifts ordinarily are "things" that people give to one another. These "things" can have important meanings attached to them. They can be signs of important human realities: love, care, thanks, thoughtfulness and so forth. But mostly we think of gifts as "things."

Faith is not a "thing." Faith is not a quantity of that thing we call grace, or even a shot of life. Faith is the name for the gift of one person to another. Faith is the gift of self, not of a thing.

We discover this when we examine what happens when any person comes to "believe in" any other person. The first step takes place when another person walks into my life in whatever way. That person is often a stranger, either because he or she comes for the first time, or because I have not paid much attention to that person before. Or it can be the other way around: I walk into someone else's life. Either way, one person takes the initiative in letting self be known. What is important is that one person initiates the possibility of further relationship and thereby opens self to the risk of acceptance or rejection.

At some point in this dynamic, there is response. If the response is positive, I begin to accept the person. I invite the other person in. I make myself open. I begin to engage in a relationship that has about it all the signs of acceptance and trust. Natural trust is the lively sign of acceptance. The relationship is beginning to be capable of belief. At this point of truth, we can say, "I accept you. I am ready to offer myself to you. I can believe in you. I can believe in what you say. I am ready to listen to you with faith and confidence." The opening has been made. The first big hurdle is overcome. The relationship grows rapidly from this point. It is, I think, a familiar experience for all of us, whether it takes place on an individual basis or in a group.

God comes to people in the same way. If we accept the validity of the human experience described above, we know exactly how to think of the "gift of faith." God always starts it. No human person can begin a faith relationship with God, ever. God always begins. That is what it means to be God. God freely offers self to all people through Jesus in the power of the Spirit. Understanding faith is to understand as fully as possible this fact: *God is freely offered to all people through Jesus in the power of the Spirit.*

When we talk about a faith relationship with God some things are altogether different and unique. The big difference is this: God does it all, literally. God always begins the experience and God carries the experience all the way through. All we can do is be open to the advances of a loving God. It is important that we know this. If we don't, we will not manage the relationship well.

Let me try to explain. Remember what we read in the Gospel of John: "God *first* loved us." So simple, so profound. God comes, God enters our life. What does that mean? How can God come, when by nature God is always there? In a real sense, God does not "come" as much as God lets us "see" divinity or "recognize" divine presence. By grace we receive the power to "see" God. In this first movement of the faith experience God is the one who makes it possible for us to experience the divine presence.

God has to do more than that if we are to move into full faith. God has to give us the power to be sure that it is God that we experience. Faith means not only that we "see" but that we are "sure." This is what the catechism calls the "certitude" of faith. In the faith experience we cannot make ourselves sure. That is God's work also.

The faith of a grown-up person must be able to live and grow comfortably with all the tough questions and doubts that are the normal predicament of any person growing from childhood through adolescence to healthy, responsible adult life.

So far, in the experience of faith, we are describing the action of God making the gift of self to us. The experience of faith is not complete, however, until we make a response. Even though this response is our movement toward God, we are not able to make it by ourselves. God has to give us the power to accept God into our lives. God has to give us the power to cry out, "I do believe." All of this, God's revealing of self and our responding, is the work of God. Remember what Paul says? "No one can say even 'Lord Jesus!' unless the Spirit gives it to him."

Can you ever forget that heartwarming moment when doubting Thomas looked up at Jesus and cried out: "My Lord and my God!" It was Jesus who gave Thomas the desire, the strength, the courage to make this complete surrender.

The only thing we can do in this faith experience is to make ourselves open enough so that God can enter in and be with us. When I say the "only" thing we can do is to be "open" I do not mean that this is an easy thing to do. It is actually difficult, because there are all kinds of forces in our lives that try to keep us closed: inherited prejudices, cultural values, influence of parents and environment, our almost overwhelming drive for security — you name it. Whatever it is works mightily to keep us captive in our tight little world. There is so much working to keep people closed that it seems a miracle for anyone to make it out of the cave.

In our own faith journey it will help to look at the way Jesus brought his disciples to faith and commitment to him and to his work. If we understand how Jesus did it when he was on earth, we can understand how Jesus does it now. There is no difference. The faith experience of the disciples is the faith experience of all those who have ever believed in Jesus, those who believe in him now and all those who will come to believe. This is true because all these full faith experiences with Jesus took place *after* the resurrection. All of them.

When Jesus was on earth in Palestine, he offered himself to people in the same way we do. He went out to them, he associated with them, he talked with them, he cried and laughed with them, he hugged them and kissed them. He went to their weddings, to their funerals and to their dinner parties. Through these ordinary and familiar human experiences Jesus made himself present; he offered himself for acceptance or rejection; *he gave of himself.* People accepted him or rejected him in as many different ways as there were individuals. Through these human experiences the Spirit of God began to reveal Jesus for who he really was to those who would become his disciples in faith.

People began to believe in Jesus because the Spirit of God, working in and through him, gave them the power to see, the urge to respond. How much did they see? How much did they respond in faith? The consensus of those who have studied the matter carefully and have pondered the evidence given to us in the scriptures say the response was minimal until after the resurrection! That was the turning point. We will look at that experience in a minute. The issue here is simple but important: the Spirit of God began calling some people to faith in Jesus *through the human signs he made, through their association with him.*

From the point of view of faith we see a remarkable difference in the conduct of the disciples before the resurrection and after the resurrection. Look at them just after Jesus had died. A more defeated, fearful, miserable bunch of people you never saw. Faith? Hope? If they had any, it is not too visible. Now look at these same people after the resurrection. Can you believe the difference? You'd better, because those same disciples are the people who got the whole thing we call Christianity going today.

"We have seen the Lord! He is risen and he is with us!" The gospel writers capture the excitement of the disciples' faith experience with Jesus after his rising. Magdalene at the tomb, the disciples in the upper room, the disciples at Emmaus — how are we to interpret these stories? What do they mean for us? One thing is absolutely certain: We see men and women transformed into new people. We see them change from defeat to victory. We see men and women who claim that they have "seen the Lord." We see men and women who are so sure they have seen the Lord that eventually they give their lives as witnesses of their sure faith. We see men and women whose faith in Jesus was so strong, so consuming a fire that they were able to change the course of history until the end of time.

The effect of Jesus' followers on world history is an overwhelming testimony to the power of faith. Nobody can ignore it. The important question for us at this point is: What really happened to them? How did it happen? The question is important because the answer we give has much to say, not only about the faith experience of the disciples, but about our own faith experience as well.

We have, in the gospels and in the Acts of the Apostles, accounts of the coming of the Spirit at Pentecost and many other times. The disciples were sure that what had happened to them was the work of the Spirit, the Spirit of Jesus. No question about that. They said it over and over again. They remembered words of Jesus, promises of Jesus, that he would have to go away, but that he would send "his" Spirit to them, to help, to lead them on. And, by their own words and actions, they claimed to be sure that what Jesus promised actually did happen. Read again the first sermons of Peter and Paul in Acts of the Apostles (2:14–36; 3:12–26; 13:16–41).

In the gospel accounts, these people spoke of Jesus appearing to them at different times and in different places. Jesus was present; they were sure of that. It was *Jesus* who was present, not someone else, not something else. Those people were filled with a sense of power and energy that they had never known and they knew it! The presence of Jesus was so real to them that the only way they could find to describe the experience was in the familiar images of the encounters they had with him before he was taken away. They saw him and they heard his voice; they touched him and they ate with him. In his presence they were brought to see and understand clearly who he was and what his mission was. In the same clarity of vision they came to see and accept who they were and what their task was to be.

Still, scripture scholars and theologians, reflecting on all this evidence, assert that all these encounters were "faith experiences." What they mean by this is that only those who were "in faith" experienced Jesus. Avery Dulles, a well-known Jesuit theologian, says that if Pontius Pilate or Josephus, the Jewish historian, had been present in the upper room, they would have seen and heard nothing. They would have experienced nothing. They were not "in faith."

Now let's look at all this from a different perspective. What do we know about the event we call the resurrection? What do we know about the risen Jesus? Not too much for sure. The one sure thing we know is that after the resurrection people were no longer able to see him or touch him with their human senses. That is the fact. Christians have reflected on that fact, speculated about that fact in light of what they knew of Jesus, in light of what he had told them about himself and about his work. From this reflection and speculation emerge some other statements that, in faith, we accept with a certainty that leaps beyond human certainty.

The risen Jesus is no longer limited to time and space. He is free. He transcends time and space. He fills the universe, all of it. Nothing of the created world is absent from his presence. He is totally present and available. This, it seems, is what it means to be risen. He is risen and he is with us!

Jesus is also "raised to glory." He is glorified. What does that mean? We use the word again and again, but do we really know what it means? For most people it spells some kind of Fourth of July spectacle. This image is not bad, but what substance does it have? To be glorified by God, to be brought from earthly existence to the full glory of God: what does it mean, really?

It means, at least, that Jesus, in being raised up, has come into full possession of his being. He has become all that he could possibly become. Nothing is lacking to his complete perfection. More than that, he has been given full possession of the Spirit. Forever he is Lord of the universe! Forever he can send forth the Spirit of God into the whole world, into the hearts and minds of all people, into the churches who are called and committed to proclaim his presence and his mission to all peoples. This is the Jesus who enters our lives in faith, the Jesus who wants in and who will not be denied.

This is the Jesus who, in the faith experience, comes to us *through us.* That is the important thing for us to know. Jesus comes to us through us. Because we can no longer see and touch his body, he designates us to be his body. Jesus has to do it that way because the only way we have of communicating is through our bodies. Jesus becomes present and available to all people in and through all people and through the created universe. Jesus is not more present and available in his church; but in church he is present and available as one who is recognized, acknowledged, celebrated and proclaimed in his own name.

The church, therefore, is the *sacrament* of Jesus. We, who are church, are his body. Ours is the face that people can recognize. Ours is the voice that other people can hear. For all time to come, until the end, we are called to be sign and witness of Jesus' presence among all people. We are called upon to make the human signs through which Jesus chooses to make himself available to people.

Isn't it weird, really? We seem to be willing, Sunday after Sunday, to worship with strangers and let them remain strangers. And we call ourselves Christian. What a wasted opportunity! What a denial of faith!

When he was on earth Jesus made good, clear signs of his desire to be present to people. In all the human signs he made, *he gave of himself.* Never did he make a sign for its own sake. Always the sign carried him to those he wanted to reach. And so the pattern is set for all time. We make the signs, good human signs, signs through which we make ourselves fully present, signs through which we *give ourselves to others*. Through these signs, Jesus, in the power of the Spirit, comes to us, reveals himself, gives us the power to see, to be sure and to respond, the power to say yes. This is what faith is all about, nothing less: a fantastic encounter with Jesus through the human signs we make, in the power of the Spirit.

The next and obvious question is this: How do we help ourselves and our people make the kind of human signs by which Jesus can attract people to himself in faith? Any old kinds of signs simply will not do. We have to make attractive signs. We are capable of making good signs and bad signs, signs that attract people and signs that turn people off. We are capable of making signs that give life or signs that take life away.

We are able, therefore, to turn people away from Jesus or to draw them to him. We can enhance the saving work of Jesus or we can cripple and thwart that work. We can make signs that increase and nourish faith or we can make signs that weaken and destroy the faith of others. That is a fact. Jesus has drawn us so very closely into a partnership with him. It is an enormous responsibility.

When we say this truth, we are *not* saying that God is limited in any way whatsoever to what is human. We are only speaking about a mystery. We are speaking about God's choice. We are speaking about the mystery of incarnation, that mystery of God's incredible design that makes us instruments of his saving work on earth.

We must realize that Jesus does not restrict himself to working only through the church. Whenever people anywhere on earth make human signs of welcome, of care, of compassion, they are caught up immediately in the work of Jesus seeking to enter the lives of people. They are instruments of Jesus' saving love. These people need not be Christians; they need not be aware of Jesus at all. They need only be doing the decent human thing. Remember the parable of the king in Matthew's gospel: "When I was in prison, you came . . . when I was hungry, you brought me food . . . but, Lord, we didn't know . . . as long as you did it to any one of my brothers and sisters, you did it to me."

So we encourage people to be concerned about their sisters and brothers, whoever they may be, wherever they are. We encourage those who believe in Jesus to be concerned and to care for brothers and sisters in the name of the Lord, because this is, above all, what it means to be a Christian. The bottom line is, always has been and always will be: love your brothers and sisters. Nothing else. The energy of passing over from this life to the reign of God is, for all people, the energy of love for brothers and sisters and service to them.

We encourage people to learn how to be open to one another and therefore open to the faith experience of Jesus coming into their lives. We ask them to be hospitable, to practice hospitality deliberately. This "hospitality" is the first and easiest step in the business of being open in faith. Hospitality asks simply that we make room in our lives for other people *while they are present.* Nothing more. Hospitality asks us to take the trouble to pay attention to others, to go out of our way to pay attention to others, while they are present. Hospitality is absolutely the first step in any effort to be open to other people. People who will not open themselves, for whatever reason, to the simple demands of hospitality are closed people. And people who close themselves off to brothers and sisters close themselves off to the Lord.

If we are serious about growing in faith, we churchgoing Catholics have to be serious about hospitality at Sunday Mass, because it is the necessary beginning of the faith experience that we want to happen at Sunday Mass.

People who help develop the experience of simple, caring hospitality at Mass on Sunday make it possible for faith life to grow by leaps and bounds. They are making a living, life-giving symbol of the hospitality of God, which is offered without any price, through Jesus, through us, in the power of the Spirit. Says God: "Come to my glorious reign. It is for you. There is room in my life and in my house for all of you. Come. Come on in."

Those who create hospitality at Mass on Sunday are breaking down the barriers that keep people from responding to God's generous invitation because by opening ourselves to one another we are opening ourselves to Jesus. And that is the necessary condition for faith. The rest of the faith encounter is up to Jesus. Jesus promised. And he is faithful.

Isn't it weird, really? We seem to be willing, Sunday after Sunday, to worship with strangers and let them remain strangers. And we call ourselves Christian. What a wasted opportunity! What a denial of faith!

In all this effort to generate the possibility of faith encounter through preaching and celebrating hospitality at the parish Sunday Mass, we need to be sensitive to the many different levels of faith among our people. These people whom God loves so much come from everywhere on the faith scale. There are those who are full of faith, bright and beaming, at times overwhelming; in their exuberance and excess they can frighten off other brothers and sisters. Then there are those who are not sure whether they believe or not, who come vaguely searching, drawn by something unknown. Still others come out of a sense of religious duty rooted primarily in fear and ignorance.

In the Sunday assembly we must be ready and able to accept members at their different levels of faith. We have to make continued signs of our thoughtfulness so that people will get the message.

You can read much more in detail about how we can generate the experience of Jesus at Mass that leads to deep and strong faith in my publication called *Giving Life: Ministry of the Parish Sunday Assembly* and in other publications.

I urge you, wherever you are in your faith journey, to develop that measure of hospitality of which you are capable. Our efforts to make ourselves available to others in care and concern, in church or out of church, creates the energy that helps people be open to the possibility of Jesus entering their lives. This is what we can *do* about faith. This is our part. The rest is the work of God through Jesus in the power of the Spirit. And God is faithful.

There are some other things about faith that adult people need to know. One of them is that faith does not have too much to do with "feeling good." Sometimes we get to feel good about God and about ourselves and about other people. Such feelings are like a bonus from the Lord or good biorhythms or both. More often than not, we do not have these good feelings. We can get discouraged, especially when we are surrounded by people who expect us to be full of joy and praising the Lord all the time.

I used to get discouraged about all this. I don't anymore. Rather, I get irritated. I believe in enthusiasm and think it is one ingredient seriously lacking, often discouraged, in the Catholic church. But not all the time, please! Let me feel bad once in a while. Don't be telling me that I have to feel good. It's like when people say to you all the time, "Have a good day." One possible response is, "Well, I really had other plans."

Also, don't be telling me the Lord will take care of everything. In the long run, I do count on him totally. At a given moment or in a given crisis, I figure I better get busy and do something about my difficulties. Just know that excellent faith, good and strong faith, does not necessarily guarantee a continual high.

Another point: Faith lives comfortably with all the usual neurotic feelings and fears we all share. Faith lives comfortably with all kinds of doubt and uncertainty, too. In fact, faith *needs* questions and doubt in order to grow. How can grown-up people possibly develop grown-up faith unless they are able to ask adult questions about values that affect their lives and about rules and regulations that affect their freedom to live as responsible adults? I do not know any genuine adult who has not been through many crises of faith.

Adults are responsible for forming their own consciences. This obligation to make decisions and to stand by them is precisely what marks the difference between adults and children. An adult cannot yield this responsibility and no one else has the right to take it away.

After a few bouts with doubt and uncertainty and rebellion, adults begin to accept the fact that faith grows in this fashion.

They begin to live calmly and productively within the faith maturing process. Most adults figure there is going to be more of the same. They are right. There *is* going to be lots more of same.

Real grown-up people learn to handle these moments mostly by keeping in touch with the people who love them as well as with those who are competent to help, to inspire, to nourish. Sometimes the lights go out. When they do, grown-ups reach out and begin to turn them on again.

One final note: faith is fragile and needs a lot of nourishment. As a person who needs to keep growing in faith I need a community of sisters and brothers who are interested in keeping my faith alive and who know they need me. I know I need them.

We have to share our faith in order to grow. Faith unshared, like life and love, starts to shrivel and decay. When we give ourselves generously and freely to others we are sharing faith, whether in everyday living or in our religious celebrations. This experience of sharing is as necessary for faith as oxygen is for breathing. When we stop breathing, we die. When we stop sharing our faith, we begin to die.

6

PRAYER OF ADULTS

There must be a million books on prayer, with many more still to come. Some of them are pretty good; more of them are bad. About all this material I have two concerns: First, since fewer than five percent read the books already published, how do ordinary, average churchgoing Catholics get to know what is important and valuable about prayer? Second, out of all the material that has been written on prayer, what should these people know in order to live as adults and grow as adults in prayer life?

I have definite answers to these questions, answers that come out of strong convictions. Perhaps my answers will be troublesome to some prayer "experts," but I cannot give them up and I want you to hear them.

There is a third question: How can average churchgoing Catholics be helped to grow and develop in adult prayer? My answer is simple and uncomplicated: the only place that these people can be reached is where they can be found, and that is at Sunday Mass.

All the important notions about adult prayer can be experienced at Sunday Mass. They need to be experienced at Sunday Mass because that's the only opportunity the average Catholic has of getting hold of them. Prayer needs to be "experienced." It is not a head trip. Knowledge alone does not bring people to prayer. Experience does — experience accompanied by reflection.

Our chief act of prayer and worship is Sunday Mass. It is rooted in the finest tradition of prayer and worship. It is prayer in its finest form. It is prayer in the biblical tradition. It is God-centered worship. It is prayer that blesses and praises and gives thanks. It is all that healthy prayer should be.

I am going to try to show, in this chapter, how all the basic energies of adult prayer can be experienced at Sunday Mass and, therefore, can be learned at Sunday Mass. I am presuming that adult churchgoing Catholics are more and more willing to take on the privilege and responsibility that is theirs by reason of baptism. My presumption is backed up by my own personal experience in many parishes in this country. This experience tells me that more and more Sunday Mass people are taking on their part of the responsibility to help develop healthy and life-giving patterns of Sunday worship.

First, some personal history will tell you where I am coming from and why I am so concerned about this issue of prayer. I hate to think that other adults might have to take the same journey that I took in order to come to some sensible attitudes about prayer and to some satisfactory patterns of prayer.

For me prayer is a victory hard won. To get there I fought dragons and witch doctors, my best friends and some of the most respected people around. I was enticed by mystical mumbo-jumbo and waylaid by all kinds of well-meaning characters. I bought lots of snake oil. I met my Buddha along the way and killed him. I was seduced into many a barren desert by the siren call of self-appointed gurus. How I escaped it all and found my way into the healthy world of the Bible I will never know. Journeys like my own make me believe fervently in the power of the Spirit.

My different prayer journeys wound up almost always in a kind of dead end, where "special people" did "special things" in order to pray. And these "special" people were always the few, the elite. I felt trapped and, in a sense, betrayed. Why does it have to be this way? Why am I asked to go through all kinds of contortions in order to do something so simple and so humanly natural as prayer? It was like being required to spend years learning how to do something as basic as breathing.

Furthermore, what about all the millions and more of God's beautiful people? Are they lost and abandoned, condemned to a life without prayer merely because they haven't time to go to the desert, because they cannot afford a guru? As a matter of fact, the deserts are either too few or too far away and gurus are getting as expensive as gasoline and as distant as Mars. Also a lot of the self-appointed gurus turn out to be quacks. I feel that we are creating two worlds: the small, snobbish world of the prayerful elite in contrast to the wide, wide world of all God's wonderful second-class citizens.

Must all these wonderful people be condemned to the kind of narcissistic navel-gazing that seems characteristic of so many schools of prayer today? Must they continue to pray "Gimme, gimme, gimme," just because they do not know any better? In this world of prayer most of our parish people are definitely second-class citizens. It is time they were released from their bondage.

Another thing happened on my journey: I got infected with Manichaeism and never knew it. Manichaeism, an old heresy that always keeps cropping up, holds that body and flesh are basically evil and that "spirit" is basically good. This infection I also call the "Platonic plague," which, by the way of the "Cartesian curse," has left us infected with the disease of "Manichaeism." Let me explain.

Plato taught simply that spirit was good, body a hindrance. The highest good for humans, therefore, was to become as "spiritual " as you could, leaving body and material things as far away as possible. The church got into the struggle early on. Evil became identified with body, good with "soul."

It is from this woefully distorted notion of the human person that we have inherited our cockeyed view of sexuality. The catechism went like this: Spirit is good. Soul is spirit. Soul is good. Body is bad. Sex is body. Sex is bad. To make matters worse, in the sixteenth century along came Descartes, swinging his mighty ax and happily sundering the human person into two distinct and separate parts, body and soul. That did it. Humpty Dumpty has not yet been put back together again. We are working on it, but it is a hard job.

That is why, my dear readers, we can talk so glibly today about our "spiritual" life and have programs for becoming "spiritual" without any reference to the flesh that we are, the bodies we bear, the whole, single and unique persons that we are. That is why we can, with clear consciences, have an intense "spiritual" life while in the same moment we can kill off brothers and sisters by the quiet violence of the arms race, discrimination, racism and monopolized wealth. It is an unhealthy climate, without room for honest-to-God, full-fleshed and full-spirited healthy people.

So let's make our way back to the healthy, life-giving world of the Bible and biblical prayer. There, we can live and move and have our being, all of it. The Semitic people of the Bible never thought of a human person as having a body and a soul. They thought always and spoke always of the one, single person, unique, not in any way capable of being separated into identifiable, separate parts.

The prayer of these people, as we find it throughout the Bible, particularly in the psalms, is a predominantly a prayer of praise and thanksgiving. All their great feasts were filled with this prayer of praise and thanksgiving. "Blessed are you . . . we praise you and we give you thanks." If there is a central characteristic of Bible prayer, it is the characteristic of praise and thanks.

So also with prayer in the early church. The public prayer of the church was rooted in synagogue worship. It comes out clear and strong as mainly praise and thanksgiving. The great official prayer of public worship in the early church, the eucharistic prayer, is a prayer of praise and thanksgiving to God for all that he has done for his people, particularly for what he has done through the work of Jesus. Into this prayer, for the sake of grateful remembering, is inserted the institution narrative, the memorial of the Lord's Supper, the memorial of Jesus' dying and rising.

There was prayer of petition in the early church also. But it was different from what we know as prayer of petition today. It was, as the Greeks would say, *epicletic:* petition to God through Jesus that the Spirit would work in the lives of the people all that God wants for them, for their good and their welfare.

In the same early church, up to about the fourth century, there was little difference between the style of the public prayer of the church — eucharist, morning and evening prayer — and the style of private prayer. The chief characteristic of private prayer was likewise praise and thanksgiving. The model of all Christian prayer was biblical prayer, prayer that placed praise and thanksgiving first and foremost. After the fourth century, things began falling apart in a number of ways. There began the separation in points of view and in worship between the eastern and western church, much of it sparked by reaction to the Arian heresy. In the western church there was the gradual segregation of clergy from people. This separation was an accomplished fact by the end of the ninth century.

The effects of the breakdown in the prayer life of the people were disastrous. Public worship became the private preserve of the clergy. The people were forgotten; they were left to shift for themselves, and so they did. Cut off as they were from any life-giving contact with the worship and sacramental life of the church, people did what people always do. They made up their own prayers and devotions. These popular prayers and devotions became largely "God and me" prayers and "gimme" prayers. Gone was the community dimension of prayer; gone was any real predominance of praise and thanksgiving. Gone was any sense of the biblical tradition of prayer.

Public prayer was confined mostly to monasteries and consequently took on, more and more, a clerical tone and color. It was clergy prayer. Later on, this breviary form of prayer continued to maintain its clerical identity and was hardly touched by the reforms of Vatican II. I am not at all convinced that this form of prayer, with its monastic overtones, is the most desirable prayer for diocesan priests today, let alone average, workaday people. The ingredients, which are the basic ingredients of all prayer, are fine. The style and pattern, however, is still unreformed monasticism.

For me prayer is a victory hard won. To get there I fought dragons and witch doctors, my best friends and some of the most respected people around. I was enticed by mystical mumbo-jumbo and waylaid by all kinds of well-meaning characters. I bought lots of snake oil. I met my Buddha along the way and killed him. I was seduced into many a barren desert by the siren call of self-appointed gurus. How I escaped it all and found my way into the healthy world of the Bible I will never know. Journeys like my own make me believe fervently in the power of the Spirit.

This somewhat schizophrenic situation is what we have inherited in our time: two kinds of prayer, each with its own emphasis. Our public worship today, if understood properly, is dominated by God and therefore characterized by praise and thanksgiving. On the other hand, private, individual prayer has come to be dominated by personal need and is therefore characterized mostly by petition. It is no wonder that the majority of our people still have difficulty coming to terms with the prayer style and demands of the new worship. It is not at all the style and form they are used to. It is neither fulfilling nor satisfying.

I am not saying that we should not ask God for our needs. I am saying that we must help people develop prayer patterns of praise and thanksgiving. Praise and thanksgiving seek God for his own sake. Prayer of petition, on the other hand, implies that God exists for us, not we for God. It becomes us to praise God because he is God, because he is who he is in himself. The first posture of adults before God is to recognize themselves as the wonderful and glorious creation of God and to profess themselves as such. An appropriate sense of sin comes later.

This is how an adult point of view differs from that of a child. Children necessarily seek their needs from all those around them and are not really capable of any other stance. Becoming an adult means separating from childhood. The final mark of truly grown-up, mature persons is a sense of responsibility to all that is outside: to God, as creator and saving Lord, and to the community as object of their life-giving energies.

Developing the prayer of praise and thanksgiving is one way of helping adults learn how to be adults and to express themselves as adults. There are some valuable helps and models at hand. The charismatic renewal, for instance, places great emphasis on praise and thanksgiving as central to all prayer. Some, but not nearly enough, of this quality of prayer is rubbing off on the whole community. We need to make that style of prayer happen more often — not the excess which this style of prayer frequently exhibits but, rather, a healthy development among Christian people. It is foolishness to turn away from the value of this prayer style simply because some people carry it to excess.

Another energy helping to bring people more readily to the stance of adult prayer in the worshiping assembly is the kind of song that is fast becoming a part of our Sunday worship. I speak both of the excellent Christian hymn tradition we have learned from our Protestant brothers and sisters and also of the music loosely (often erroneously) called "folk." The latter form of music, from our better composers, is very much Bible centered. Notice the strong tendency to psalm paraphrase. Here we have an important development in making public prayer become what it is supposed to be. The song-prayers used at Mass today offer excellent ways for learning how to pray as adults. I think we must call attention to this fact. People haven't noticed it enough.

Since the reform and renewal of Vatican II the average Sunday churchgoer is being nourished on a diet of scriptural prayer and scriptural image as never before in parish history. And the people love it. Even snobbish music reviewers can't keep them from claiming these songs and making them their own favored form of expression.

There is what I would call an urgent need to help our adult community at Sunday Mass learn more about the kind of prayer they are being invited to share with one another. At the same time we need to offer them the best models. The eucharistic prayer itself, even in its still undeveloped form, is the finest model we have. It will be even more valuable when it gains the kind of development that is promised and when members of the parish Sunday assembly begin to understand what the prayer is all about.

In order to make this great prayer of the eucharist available to people, we have to get rid of some false theological presuppositions. From what we hear, we are led to think that this prayer is the priest's private preserve: Let no one dare enter. The eucharistic prayer is *not* the "priest's prayer" in this sense at all. The eucharistic prayer is the prayer of the church. The priest, as leader of the assembly, is deputed to lead this prayer. To him belongs the role of chief celebrant or presider (whichever you wish). His task in leading this prayer is to engage the whole community. He should use voice, face, eyes and gesture to draw people into the prayer. If he does not draw them into it, he fails badly in his task as leader.

It is also false theology to say that, since this prayer is addressed to the Father, the priest must not look at the people but to God. That seems to mean looking upward. Yes, the prayer is addressed to the Father — that is clear enough — but it is a story told for the sake of the assembly. It is the prayer of the entire assembly. That's the whole point! God is not hovering somewhere in the ceiling.

In order to make this great prayer available to our people, the priest-celebrant needs to inspire them and lift their eyes from the written text while he proclaims it. If people read along, they are effectively cutting themselves off from any real experience of the prayer. Priests must learn to proclaim this prayer in such a way that it would be difficult for people not to become engaged in it. Finally, priests must preach this eucharistic prayer, taking time and helping people to understand what it is all about, where it comes from, what the different parts are, and how they all fit together. This can be stunning and life-giving material for Sunday homilies. "We must," wrote Gilbert K. Chesterton, "look at familiar things until they become strange again." Parish people ought to be knocking on the rectory door and clamoring for this kind of enlightened and enlightening homily.

On the other hand, adults at Sunday Mass are not spectators to the prayer and action of someone else "way up there." They must become active in this prayer. The presider "way up there" should be the storyteller. The people "way out there" should be listening to the storyteller tell the story. Even if the storyteller is not doing a good job in telling the story, adults still have the responsibility to put themselves into the prayer as much as possible. This is the prayer of the entire assembly. Everybody must be involved if the prayer is to become the living and life-giving experience it is supposed to be. We can't put all the blame on the priest.

If adults are to continue to grow in prayer, they must also get a chance to learn about contemplative prayer. In order to learn it and make it their own, they must experience it. Sunday Mass provides the only possible opportunity for most Catholics to experience contemplative prayer. Catholic adults need to know that contemplative prayer is easy and can be practiced by anybody at any time. They need to give the lie to the popular impression that contemplative prayer is something that can be done only by special people in special places, using special methods.

Nothing could be further from the truth. The contemplative experience is the natural prayer of all human persons. People do it all the time, unaware that they are doing it. With just a little more understanding of its meaning, people would be able to engage more and more often, more and more deliberately in the contemplative experience. It is truly adult fare. We should no longer be hiding natural contemplative prayer from our people.

In every Sunday Mass we have right at hand all the ingredients necessary for the members of the assembly to experience this most delightful and satisfying form of prayer.

In order to bring about this happy state of affairs, two things have to happen on Sunday at Mass: experience and reflection. Both must happen at the same time. Experience without reflection can produce a high that doesn't usually last any longer than it takes to get out of church.

Sunday Mass affords the best of all opportunities to put experience and reflection together. This is so because Sunday worship is, in its very nature, a contemplative act, a contemplative experience. This same contemplative experience is the most important wellspring of genuine discipleship.

The act of contemplation always begins from the outside. God comes to us through our experience with the created world, particularly through our experience with each other. This is the most basic truth of our relationship with God. Every time we depart from that anchor, we lose our bearings and start wandering off in many different and often foolish directions.

To be truly human means simply that each of us is a person: one, inseparable, unique. This means that whatever comes to us, whoever comes to us, comes through the only accessible opening we have, our senses. There are no other hidden ways of getting in. God made us this way and respects what he has made. God deals with humans as they are. God comes the way he needs to come, because that is how he can get to us.

God comes to his people through the human experiences they share. This is the outstanding characteristic of the entire history of God's dealing with his people. Examine the history of our biblical ancestors, particularly their Exodus experience. Examine the personal experience of Jesus, as far as we are able to penetrate that mystery. Examine the experience of the first disciples as it is related in Scripture, particularly the Acts of the Apostles. Examine your own personal experiences.

So the beginning of all prayer is outside of us. The process goes something like this: The outside world — all creation, things and people — begins to make us what we will become, long before we know about it or think about it. To everything outside of us, we make some kind of response. It is the very nature of any living organism to respond to its environment. An infant begins the learning process in the womb. (Education is another thing and begins later.)

The contemplative experience is the natural prayer of all human persons. People do it all the time, unaware that they are doing it. With just a little more understanding of its meaning, people would be able to engage more and more often, more and more deliberately in the contemplative experience. It is truly adult fare. We should no longer be hiding natural contemplative prayer from our people.

In the beginning of the contemplative experience there is little or no awareness of what is going on. It's like being at the seashore. First, we are just there, without thinking about it. Then suddenly we become aware. We realize that something is happening to us. We begin to pick up the vibrations that have begun sometime before we recognize them. We discover beginnings of response welling up from inside: wonder, delight, fear, excitement and all the others. If, through this experience, God has chosen to make his presence felt, we begin somehow to sense a presence. We begin to have a feeling that there is *more* here than we are in touch with. That feeling is often vague and unclear. That doesn't make any difference. God is a mystery. God is not clear to us. The important reality is that God is making himself available to us.

If we are open enough and if God so chooses, we begin to call the presence we are experiencing by the name of God. This is particularly true if we already have some notions of God and Jesus. We feel ourselves being pulled out of ourselves by the strength and power of someone else. God is beginning to give us the ability to recognize him and the power to be sure that it is God we are experiencing. We begin to hold the experience. We begin to examine it. We begin to taste it. We begin to be filled with it, with *someone.* We find ourselves coming up with a word. The word grows and grows within until finally it explodes, "God is in this holy place! Praise the Lord! Bless his name!" We name God as the one who has entered our life, and we respond to him with a grateful "Yes." We yield. We let God take over.

Perhaps the above is not the most elegant description of prayer you have ever heard. Poets and saints have done it better, both Christian and non–Christian. I suggest, though, that you read it again and think about some of your own personal experiences. You will begin to discover and understand what has happened to you many times.

Remember the times you were singing a song in church at an important celebration, and you suddenly had to stop because you were going to cry? Remember moments of loss of a loved one, moments of grief, moments of pain and recall how the experience suddenly took you over. You were lifted beyond yourself, outside yourself. (This is, by the way, what the word ecstasy means. It comes from the Greek *ekstasis* and means standing outside yourself.) The whole experience is simple and at the same time profoundly mysterious. We are in touch with what is "out there" and then something "happens."

That is the whole point. Something, someone "happens" to us. We don't do it; we don't make it happen. We can't make it come or go away. It happens, and then we respond. If Jesus is reaching out to us in one or other of these experiences to bring us more deeply into relationship with himself, he will, through the power of the Spirit, make clear to us what he wants and lead us further on. Examine the experience of Saint Paul on his way to Damascus. This is exactly what happened to him. And notice, please, that no one else knew what was happening. This experience was for him alone, not for anyone else. Paul's response, our response, is the beginning of prayer.

Prayer is always a response. God begins the action. We make a response to God's prompting. If we know these truths about prayer and can accept them, we have a better idea of what to do and what not to do in prayer. We know we cannot make God reveal himself, so we don't try. And we don't get all bent out of shape if he does not reveal himself. We know that all we can do, the best we can do, is to be open and to fashion a receptive environment. We ready ourselves for the possibility. And then we wait. This is how we manifest our openness.

Our faith tells us God is there. We are sure of that. And so we are willing to wait, and to wait again. When clouds hide the sun from us, we know the sun continues to shine but we cannot see it. We never say the sun is not there. We know we cannot change the barriers between ourselves and the sun so we go on about our business, knowing the sun will be with us again when it is possible.

Sunday Mass gives us the opportunity to create an experience of contemplative prayer that can be shared by the entire assembly. Sunday Mass provides also a chance to reflect on that experience. Remember the rule: say in words only what you have to say so that people can recognize the occasion and enter into the experience. Then, provide the experience. Afterwards, reflect on the experience. If you say too much beforehand, you kill the experience. If you fail to reflect, the experience will vanish without a trace.

Here I would like to offer some thoughts on the possibility of the contemplative experience at Sunday Mass within the context of the liturgy of the word. The liturgy of the word begins with speaking the word and hearing the word. The reader speaks the word, and the listeners hear the word. In a sense this is one single act because a word is not a word unless it is heard. The word which the reader speaks is God's word. If the reader really proclaims that word with life and energy, if the reader proclaims the word with meaning and feeling and if the hearers of the word are really listening, then remarkable things begin to happen.

All members of the assembly realize that they are sharing the word not only with the reader but with one another. Sparks move from person to person. Flesh is ignited from flesh. God is speaking; the Spirit is moving. Stirrings and movements in many hearts all together are caught up into the living, life-giving presence of God. People are helping people to experience this moment of contemplative prayer. Even coughing and other unneeded noises stop. People do not want to disturb others.

The response is well underway. Members of the assembly, at whatever level they are, begin to hear as if for the first time, tasting and savoring God's word and letting it grow inside them. The experience is much like the birthing experience. Members of the assembly are receiving the seeds of God's word which grows fast within them.

That's why it is so essential to make room for some silence after the hearing of God's word. We need silence, so that we can savor and taste and nourish the response that we find welling up within us. Silence is necessary immediately after the reading. How much? It is hard to say. Enough but not too much. I figure about thirty seconds or so. During the silence, members of the assembly close their eyes and talk with the Lord about the word they have just received. "Lord, I am listening. I want to hear. Help me to be open to your message today." And so on. However it happens, that's when the contemplative experience occurs.

The responsorial psalm is part of the contemplative experience. It provides the assembly with a word to sing just when they need to respond. The church places a song on the lips of the assembly so that they can cry out the wonder of their encounter with God. The members of the assembly become bound together in their song response just as they were bound together in the listening and in the silence that followed.

Do you see how important it is to sing the response rather than recite it? It is, by its very nature, a song. It is not another reading. Only by way of exception should it be recited. Recitations succeed mostly in bleeding all life out of the response, leaving it as much energy as a collapsed balloon.

It does take time and trouble and patience to make it all happen at each Mass, each Sunday, week after week. It does not always work perfectly, but that's no reason to stop trying. God's designs for this assembly and for each precious person in this assembly are indeed a mystery. God does not always share these plans. That is God's business. We can trust God.

From this experience of prayer shared by everyone, it is

rather easy for people to go on to private prayer and work out the possibility of the same or similar experience. It works the same way. Always start outside self with a long, loving look at the real. If you haven't got time, a short loving look will do nicely. Most usually, since we want to make contact with Jesus, or with God through Jesus, we reach for the Bible. The Bible is out there, outside ourselves. We read God's word, often aloud. When we read it aloud we have a better chance to hear it, a better chance to take it in from the outside.

We read as much or as little as we wish. In this particular reading of the word we are not out to learn something. We are reaching for personal contact, so how much or how little we read makes no difference. Usually, the idea is to read until something really "strikes" us from the outside. At that point we stop, we taste, we savor, we say it over again. And then we let happen what may. We reflect for a brief moment, or for many moments. We become silent.

Often in prayer, as with persons we love, there are times when there is no further need for words. So we stop using words. We simply hold ourselves in wordless presence. We hold ourselves, or are held, in wordless presence for only as long as it lasts. When the moment is over, we know it. We do not linger, we do not regret, we do not try to go back and recapture. We are grateful for the gift and we move on. Maybe there's some time left. So we pick up the scriptures and go further along with the text. Maybe what happened the first time will happen again. Maybe not. It doesn't make much difference.

Let me tell you about an experience I had years ago. I used to find time on summer afternoons to go into our yard at Paca Street Seminary, a kind of oasis in the middle of downtown Baltimore. My intent was to make some time for prayer. I would do a variety of things to begin. Sometimes I would sit in the sun, close my eyes and begin recalling something of what I knew about Jesus, and let it happen from there. Other times I would begin to say part of the rosary quietly, trying to recall the mysteries, the important events of Jesus' life.

This particular summer I decided to begin praying with the letter to the Ephesians, which somehow had caught my fancy. So I began to read some few sentences of this exciting letter. Quickly I found myself getting involved in the very kind of contemplative process I've been describing here. It was a great and rewarding experience and still stands out in my life. After two or three weeks I was still caught in the first two chapters of Ephesians. I would read some sentences one day and, because I was so enchanted with what I had read that day, I would read the same thing over again the next day. So it went. For me it remains a kind of perfect example of what I am trying to say here and now.

In presenting these thoughts, I am not trying to take any stand on other forms or methods of praying or contemplating. I am offering what I know to be the most ancient form of prayer in the Christian church. This is prayer that begins with hearing and receiving the word of God and ends by being caught up, even momentarily, in the personal experience of God through Jesus in the power of the Spirit. For many centuries, the church's term for this kind of prayer has been *lectio divina,* Latin for a loving, receptive reading and hearing of the word of God. It is a good way, open to anybody who wants to experience it. All you need is a community that learns to cherish and nourish the word of God proclaimed in the assembly. When you are by yourself, or with another, or in a small group, all you need is a Bible.

As I see it, this apprenticeship in genuine prayer has to happen at Mass on Sunday. If we do not work to make it happen there, most of our people are going to be deprived of the transforming power and delight of adult prayer. They have no other way of getting hold of it, of being initiated into it.

7

SIN AND RECONCILIATION

God loves everybody all the time. This correct idea of God, the real God of reconciling love, is the only notion of God that allows adults to discover the true meaning of sin and reconciliation.

Our questions are simple and straight: What must we believe about sin and reconciliation? How can we help one another break the chains of guilt that have so long kept us bound, helpless and hopeless, in fear and self-condemnation? How can we celebrate the new rite of reconciliation most fruitfully as we move into the light and the warmth of the reformed and renewed sacrament? What can we learn about sin and reconciliation so that we can begin to act like grown-up people, make our own responsible decisions and stand accountable for those decisions before God and other people?

At this moment in the church we very much need proper understanding both of sin and of reconciliation in our lives. We need also to learn how to celebrate reconciliation in our lives. The healing and conversion we so desperately need comes to us through the *experience* of reconciliation.

The adults I know are crying out that they are not children and will not be treated as children any longer. They are angry and resentful against those who would keep them children forever. They do not want or need answers. They want clear knowledge and clear guidelines. Entirely capable of making their own responsible decisions, they are already making those decisions. They are bound and determined to do what marks them as adults and precisely distinguishes them from children: to make free, responsible choices. They accept gratefully their own precious God-given freedom to make their own choices and to stand by them. They want help and know that they need it. They are asking for help. At the same time they insist on being accepted as adults and being respected for the choices they make.

What help do they need? All grown-up people who would deal with sin and reconciliation in a grown-up manner need an accurate notion of the role of God, of Jesus and of the church in the work of sacramental reconciliation. They need an accurate notion of sin. They need an accurate notion of the sacrament of reconciliation and how it works. These are the guidelines they need.

FORGIVING LOVE

For adults there is only one God: the God of forgiving love, the God of Jesus Christ. All God's love, all the movement of God toward his people, is the work of reconciling. Paul says it clearly: "All this is done by God, who through Christ changed us from enemies into his friends, and gave us the task of making others his friends also. Our message is that God was making friends of all people through Christ. God did not keep an account against them of their sins, and he has given us the message of how he makes them his friends." (2 Corinthians 5:18,19)

God's love for his chosen people is, by definition, forgiving love. It really cannot be any other kind. God does not love us because we are good or when we are good. God loves everybody all the time. This correct idea of God, the real God of reconciling love, is the only notion of God that allows adults to get to the true meaning of sin and reconciliation. If adults do not break through to this notion of God, they will continue to be held prisoner by harmful and destructive notions of sin.

So it must be with the adult image of Jesus. Adults need to know that all the loving sacrificial work of Jesus is essentially the work of reconciliation. They need to know Jesus is already at work, always at work, on his mission of mercy — his rescue mission, if you wish. Jesus is about the business, all the time, of freeing all people from their hopeless and helpless bondage of human weakness, of human selfishness, of their own self-made mess of sin. Jesus is working all the time to lift them up, to heal their brokenness, to help them make peace with one another and to bring them all, a people rescued and made whole, back to the Father. That's the whole story. That's the good news about reconciliation. There is a way back, and the way is Jesus!

Jesus has called the church to be about the same mission of reconciliation. The church exists precisely to proclaim the good news of Jesus' saving work. The church is put into the world to help people identify the full meaning in Jesus of all human care and forgiveness and compassion wherever they find it. More than that, the church is called to carry on the reconciling work of Jesus in the world. The chief work of the church is to make peace, to bring justice, to lift up the broken, take them home and heal them, to search out the alienated and to make them feel secure and wanted. What greater Christian service is there than helping to reconcile a broken world? The church in the world must be the sign of the reconciling savior and an instrument of that same savior.

NOTION OF SIN

Adults need also a correct notion of sin. This is a tough one to work out. When it comes to sin we have some badly screwed-up ideas. In addition, we are riddled with unnecessary guilt, wandering around in those dark caves of the psyche opened up by Freud and others. Now that the church has made peace with psychology, we have better light to see by. A dramatic sign of the development of the church's thought and practice in the theology of sin and reconciliation is the move from the dark coffin-like box of the confessional to the well-lighted and gracious reconciliation room. Even the name change is significant: from "confession" to "reconciliation"; from "sacrament of penance" to "reconciliation rite." Grown-up people must get to know the theology of sin that is an essential part of this renewal.

Sin: Against People, Not Laws. Sin is not breaking a law. Sin is against people, not against things or concepts or structures. Sin is against life, against creation and therefore against God. Mostly, sin is against people. Sin is a breaking or rupturing or weakening of the God-given love we have with brothers and sisters. It is our duty to care for and serve brothers and sisters. Being human and being obliged to care for brothers and sisters is one and the same thing. Furthermore, the same obligation is solemnly expressed and laid upon us by God's covenant. The covenant binds us to God and to one another at one and the same time. The "great commandment" of love makes this quite clear.

Then Jesus takes the whole matter a light-year leap ahead. No longer is it enough to love brothers and sisters as you love yourself; you are supposed to love brothers and sisters as God loves them. This is the clear command of the gospel. This command is impossible, hopelessly impossible. Our native selfishness makes it so. Were it not for the fact that God gives us a share in his own life and love, we would be helpless failures. God gives us his own power to love the way he does.

When we sin, we begin to destroy other people and ourselves at the same time. When we sin, we bring about a condition in our lives and in society that we call evil. We destroy the bonds of peace and justice. We try to possess people as property and to manipulate them to our own ends. We spread fear and hatred and violence. Just by ignoring people, just by refusing to acknowledge their presence, we can wipe them out. By such conduct we are saying: you are not worth my while, even for a moment.

95

How quickly and easily and unknowingly we can spread evil and bring havoc into the lives of other people.

Sin: Fundamental Selfishness. It is at this point that we put our finger on what evil really is in all its ugliness. It is selfishness pure and simple — or, rather, not so pure and not so simple. Evil is preoccupation with self so that we no longer pay attention or care about anyone outside. Basic evil is self-centeredness. Basic good is generosity: being open and being outgoing to others. I am talking about how we choose to live, not about an intellectual position. Radical evil is being closed. Radical good is being open.

We begin to sin when we begin to choose self-centeredness deliberately. We become sinful to the degree that we deliberately turn inward and cut ourselves off from others. On the other hand we become good, or holy, to the degree that we become fully human. We become fully human when we work to develop our talents and gifts to their fullest capacity in service to others.

All of this becoming fully human, and therefore fully good, takes place most of all through personal relationship, the only way for a human person to grow and mature. Personal relationship gives us the chance to open up, to go out of ourselves to others. What a power for growth! What a power for good and evil! To the extent we deny this possibility, we do not grow up, remaining closed and shriveled up inside. In addition, when we fail to go out to others, we destroy other people and ourselves in the process.

Sin: A Private Affair? For many centuries we have been led to think of sin only as a personal and private affair: nobody's business but mine and God's. There is a clear historical reason for this. It started to happen back in the sixth and ninth centuries when sacraments became the exclusive preserve of the clergy and the community dimension of sacraments got cut off. Just

about the time that the community lost its rightful place in celebrating eucharist, it lost its rightful part in celebrating all the
other sacraments, particularly the sacrament of reconciliation.
That's when the priest emerged as the only minister of all the
sacraments. The entire sacramental life was reduced to one, single, totally vertical relationship: the individual to the priest to
God, and God back through the priest to the individual.

Private confession to a priest in a dark and anonymous box
became the symbol that said it all. Sin came to be regarded as
an entirely private and personal matter between the individual
and God with the priest as mediator.

It is safe to say that the reduction of the sense of sin to the
private and personal helped unleash the ugly monster of
Manichaeism. When self became the entire focus of attention,
the body came to be considered the source of evil, the enemy of
all that is good and spiritual. The simple adjective "carnal" became synonymous with bad and unclean. Hence sex became
number one on the hit parade of sins and seems to cling to this
spot even today. Sexual sins are regarded by many people as *the*
mortal sins. Murder makes a serious showing sometimes but
doesn't seem to have much staying power. The same is true for
injustice and all the other really evil things.

Institutional Evil. With such intense focus on personal sin
and the priority given to the evil of flesh, it is easy to see how
what we call institutional evil was simply overlooked. We still
overlook it, but there have always been individual voices from all
sides calling us to look at the evil around us. In recent decades,
voices of church leaders everywhere have been raised to decry
the evil that is caught and held in the social institutions of culture, civilization, church, politics and government. However,
despite the growing tradition of clearly targeted social encycli-
cals, we seem not yet to grasp that these are messages about

radical evil and sinfulness rooted in society and in the institutions of society.

As the level of social consciousness is raised, we witness growing protests in all the areas of social justice and institutional evil: racial and minority discrimination, disproportionate wealth or poverty, abuse of power, political corruption and dirty tricks, international exploitation and secret societies built upon hatred. Even while these voices are raised, we do not seem to grasp the intensity of the institutional evil that is alive in the world. In the same moment in which the media stuns us with the savage violence of people struggling to free themselves from racial oppression, we seem not to be disturbed by the equally savage, though quieter, violence of unconscionable poverty, apartheid and government oppression of all kinds. Sadly, the list can go on and on.

In this country the church has managed to exist at the parish level with little response to the claims of the poor and the weak and the hungry and the outcasts. I grew up in an exemplary parish. In all my years there, even beyond ordination, we managed pretty well to ignore their cry. We even regarded their "demands" as intrusion. Our conscience, both individual and collective, was not really disturbed.

Thank God, things have begun to change in our time. There is a growing awareness of the duty and responsibility for parishes to reach out to the poor and needy. Outreach of some kind is becoming an accepted, even important, part of parish life and ministry.

But we have a long way to go. Parish members, by and large, still think that the parish exists to serve the needs of those who belong to the parish. They are not yet aware that they themselves *are* the parish and therefore exist to serve the needs of each other, and, even more, the needs of those outside. The word that Jesus sent back to John still holds true as an ultimate measure of selfishness and sinfulness: "Go back and tell John what you are hearing and seeing: the blind can see, the lame can walk, the lepers are made clean, the deaf hear, the dead are raised to life, and the good news is preached to the poor." (Matthew 11:4–5)

If we are going to gain adult stature in our Christian world, we need to struggle for a balanced sense of sin in our lives. For most adults this means a development of social consciousness such as we have just described. There is really no other way to go about growing up. Adults are the ones responsible for making and keeping healthy communities. Children, or those who remain grown children, cannot do that. Adults give signs of their maturity when they measure out a balance between personal and social evil and begin to assume responsibility for the latter as well as the former. There are signs of healthy changes happening, but the scene is not changing nearly enough.

It should come as no surprise that too many adults make the same kind of confession they made when they were children. The tragedy is that too many of us so-called grownups are still willing to settle for some childish ideas of sin.

GAINING A HEALTHY NOTION
OF RECONCILIATION

Gospels: The Parables. Along with our struggle to get a truly adult sense of sin, we need also to work for a clearer idea of what reconciliation is all about. To do this we must move from unhealthy preoccupation with self into the brilliant landscape of the gospel.

It is there that we can discover again what genuine forgiveness is all about. It is there that we can find out the true meaning of genuine reconciliation. The parables! The stories of the father of the prodigal son, of Jesus and the woman taken in adultery, of Jesus and the woman at the well, the account of the good Samaritan and Jesus' advice to Peter about forgiveness. In all these and other stories, it shines out bright and clear that reconciliation is people reaching out and touching other people with forgiving love. People welcome other people into their lives. The people who are welcomed respond with joyful acceptance. They feel restored, renewed, refreshed. They are healed, forgiven, made whole again.

Sin is not breaking a law. Sin is against people, not against things or concepts or structures. Sin is against life, against creation and therefore against God. Mostly, sin is against people. Sin is a breaking or rupturing or weakening of the God-given love we have with brothers and sisters.

Reconciliation as Human Experience. We need to look carefully at what can and should happen in the experience of reconciliation in *all* moments of human forgiving, particularly in the sacramental rite of reconciliation. What really goes on there? On the one hand, we see a person who comes with some sense of sin, some sense of human infidelity. They are hurting, frustrated, discouraged, disintegrated in some way or other. They feel bad and want to do something about it. They are searching for healing.

On the other hand we have a person who is there to offer clear human signs of loving care, concern and forgiveness. It is through the human signs of this reconciling encounter — words and actions of faith, hope and love made by representatives of God and the community — that the experience of the forgiving love of God and the community is unleashed. Through these signs people actually feel loved and accepted and healed in the presence of the community and the Lord. It is like being restored to life, like being born again. That is what the sacramental experience is supposed to be all about. Everything in the rite of reconciliation is set to help this experience take place. There is no magic in any sacramental action.

The ingredients are simple: call and response. In the call, someone reaches out, touches and welcomes, in forgiving love without judgment. In the response, someone gratefully enters into the welcoming, non-judgmental forgiveness. The encounter is always personal, never superficial or mechanical. Reconciliation is possible precisely because there are clear signs of this call and response. Fences are broken down, brokenness is mended, hearts are opened and healing takes place. The heart of all reconciliation is the shared human experience of care and love. Without this shared experience, it is doubtful how much reconciliation can actually take place.

Reconciliation as Sacrament: What Happens? Since
the sacrament of reconciliation is precisely about forgiveness, we need to ask a more fundamental question: does God forgive sin at the moment of absolution and because of absolution? Has sin remained firmly unforgiven up to that precise moment? The answer is a firm *No*. This answer is contrary to popular understanding. Most people think that God wipes the slate clean in that one moment so that they can go out and make a fresh start. Here we have to avoid the "trap," understandable as it may be, of making God's forgiving love into a response dependent on what we humans do. The incredible mystery of God's ever-forgiving love cannot be made contingent upon human activities or ritual gestures. God's love is essentially forgiving from the start. Our sacraments do not make God's forgiving love *happen*. It can't happen at that precise moment, because it has already happened. When we enter into the rite we already stand forgiven before God. This is the only way we can understand God's unconditional love.

If that is the case, then what does happen in those moments of sacramental reconciliation? The same thing happens here as happens in any sacramental action: Jesus, in the power of the Spirit and through the human signs we make, reveals his saving and healing presence. Through those same human signs and in the same power of the Spirit, we make our response of faith.

Through the reconciling signs we make, we celebrate the wonder of God's forgiving love. We are exalted to a new awareness of God's forgiving love; we enter into the center of God's forgiveness; we respond to the revelation of God's love with a fresh energy of thanks and praise and admiration; we are helped by other people to discover and experience God's forgiving love. We are "converted"; we are changed in thought and attitude and feeling. We have new heart to repent more deeply and to get up and begin again. We feel accepted, affirmed, loved, forgiven. We get the courage to make clear signs of our repentance to whomever it is due. We look with fresh wonder and grateful amazement at God's most gracious love. Like the blind man, when he saw again, we go out with new energy to make peace and keep peace with sisters and brothers. This is what can happen and does happen in a fruitful celebration of the sacrament of reconciliation.

Conversion: A Continuing Process. Any single act of reconciliation does not stand alone. It cannot. It is a moment, often a significant moment, in the long process we call "conversion." One of the real difficulties with the "Sacrament of Penance," as we have known it until recently, is that we imagined we could somehow condense a whole process of conversion into a few moments within that dark and private box. The fact that we were quite content with such a process suggests just how naive we have been about the whole thing.

Before the sixth century, in the church experience to which the reforms of Vatican II are calling us back, reconciliation was understood and valued in its full dimension. The process of reconciliation went hand in hand with the process of conversion. It was expected to take time, lots of time, as does any healing process. Later, when it got all stuffed together into a single, brief, impersonal encounter, we lost sense of the time it takes for reconciliation to become fruitful. We came close to thinking about confession as a magical process without realizing what we were doing. Reconciliation can never be reduced to the expectation that its main purpose is to get "cleaned up" so that we can go to communion on Sundays.

Any conversion process starts always with seeing things differently. When someone or something enters my life and challenges me to look at myself all over again, I begin to see myself differently. I am moved to do something about it. Maybe for the first time I sense a kind of selfishness that I have been comfortable with for a long time. I see it for the first time. I do not like what I see. I feel guilty. I want to do something about it. This kind of guilt is healthy; it is not destructive neurotic guilt. It is a healthy guilt. It moves me to action. I am on the way. I am beginning the process of changing my behavior. Though I was content with myself before, now I want to change. The power of the Spirit is moving me further on the way to conversion, moving me to a better way of life.

More and more people are coming to engage in the sacrament of reconciliation in this spirit. I am talking, of course, about the people who come to the sacrament because they have been awakened to the fact they need to be reconciled and they need an "experience" of that reconciliation. While many still come from force of habit or from a vague sense of guilt or obligation, more people are coming to the sacrament because they really want to come.

QUIET REVOLUTION

There has been a *quiet revolution* by Catholic people in actual confession practice. All over the world people in great numbers suddenly stopped going to confession. No crusading call went out, no shot was fired, no reasons were given. All at once, the long lines vanished; priests sitting in confessionals experienced long breaks between confessions. This remarkable phenomenon has something important to tell us today as we work to renew the sacrament of reconciliation. Moved by this obvious revolution, the church, in putting into practice the decisions of the Second Vatican Council, took a fresh look at the entire scene of the "sacrament of penance." As a consequence we have a recovered theology of reconciliation and new rites for reconciliation.

Other interesting things have happened in this same uprising. After the "revolution," many of the people who kept coming to confession came with a different attitude. Priest-confessors began to notice that these people were quite clearly assuming the responsibility of making up their own consciences before they came. The people who came showed up with decisions already made about what they were going to tell and what they were not going to tell. The "laundry list" of sins became shorter and less specific. In the area of sexual morality it became obvious that people, particularly married people, were making up their own minds about what is and is not sinful and that they just were not dwelling on these things any more.

At the same time perceptive confessors were accepting the situation as it was presented to them. They called a halt to the demeaning practice of asking too many questions and of trying to pry out detailed information.

All this is a healthy sign of the maturing process going on among many priests and people. Adults are beginning to think like adults and act like adults.

CELEBRATING THE RITE OF RECONCILIATION

The name change for this sacrament reveals immediately the vast difference of emphasis between the old and the new. We do not need intense theological investigation to grasp the sweeping difference between celebrating reconciliation and "penance."

Because many adult Catholics have personally rejected the old habit of frequent private confession, we are presented with a historically unique challenge. We are called to be part of the process of developing patterns for celebrating the new Rite of Reconciliation. It is not enough to rely on our priests to "sell" us on the new rite. All adults in the church have a responsibility to do all we can to develop patterns of celebration that will touch people for decades to come. We have the chance to help form a fresh, living tradition.

Our first responsibility is to understand the reformed rite. Second is the responsibility to create the finest possible celebration of the rite. And finally we must join in the celebration actively and "on purpose," not only for our own sakes but even more for the sake of others.

Sacramental Principles. All those involved with developing celebrations of this sacrament need to know that the experience of reconciliation is the heart of the sacramental encounter. The goal for celebrating all forms of the rite should be to create the finest possible experience of the rite.

Those whose business it is to develop the details of this new rite need to be familiar with the basic principles of sacramental theology. Sacraments are not things. Sacraments are the personal actions of those who celebrate them. "The personal presence" of those who celebrate is the energy that makes the sacrament effective. To the degree that this personal presence is freely offered and experienced, the sacrament is effective and fruitful. To the degree that this personal presence is withheld, the sacrament becomes less fruitful. The signs we make in the reconciliation rite must be humanly attractive and expressive.

The priest-confessor needs to put people at ease immediately, which means he must be at ease himself. He needs to be gracious, relaxed, attentive. He must not be afraid to express what he has to say throughout the rite in simple and personal language, rather than in stilted and stereotypical formulas. This holds true as well for the formula of absolution.

Another point: All sacramental signs are revelatory. They are special moments when the Spirit of Jesus is busy helping us to see more clearly what we need to see at the moment. For this reason the signs of the sacrament of reconciliation must be developed in such a way that they help bring about a twofold revelation: deeper insight into our real sinfulness and the growing awareness of an ever-loving, ever-forgiving God.

Recognizing Sin. Those who develop celebrations of this rite must see to it that the encounter, whether one-to-one or communal, helps to uncover the sin in our lives that is not yet clearly recognized. Through the signs they make, the participants of the rite should be able to help one another search the heart in openness, humility and honesty. Together they help one another discover the furtive sin, the twisted heart, the crooked way, the unknown and unexpected evil that does so much damage.

In this light it becomes clear how useless is the "sin list" that for years we used to draw up so painstakingly. The sins we know are often not the most damaging. The sin we do not know is often the cancer that eats away at our guts and the guts of others. It is precisely the experience of good personal encounter in the actual celebration that helps generate the light to see more clearly and the willingness to accept what we discover.

Likewise it is through the signs of love and acceptance that are unleashed during the celebration that God reveals his saving love. Through the signs of compassion and acceptance that members of the celebration extend to each other, God lets us feel his healing love. The design of the celebration makes it possible for the participants to offer unmistakable signs of mutual love, mutual acceptance, mutual forgiveness. The celebrating community should be able to offer an embrace of care and concern, the care and concern of a sinful community working hard to cherish people in their deepest misery and in their greatest joy. These are the signs through which the Spirit of Jesus sets people free from the bondage of sin.

Counselor or Reconciler? It is in this setting that the priest-celebrant finds his new role, particularly in the one-to-one encounter. He tries to embody, in his person and in the signs he makes, those feelings and values that are so important for reconciliation: human care, concern, acceptance, affirmation. He shows these healing energies in his face, in his words and in his gestures.

The incredible mystery of God's ever-forgiving love cannot be made contingent upon human activities or ritual gestures. God's love is essentially forgiving from the start. Our sacraments do not make God's forgiving love happen. It can't happen at that precise moment, because it has already happened.

He is no longer the faceless and impersonal judge. Rarely is he called upon to make judgments about the worthiness or unworthiness of people. Most of the time he is called upon to help people form their own judgments, not to make their judgments for them. I had no trouble giving up this role of judge. I find the new role of fellow sinner and compassionate minister marvelously and beautifully overwhelming and infinitely healing, as much for myself as for others.

The issue of the priest-confessor role versus the priest-counselor role has been debated back and forth for a long time. In our own time, it becomes clear that the reconciliation room is for sacramental encounter, not for counseling. Counseling, most of the time, is best done elsewhere and, for the most part, by a different person. The counselor role and the reconciler roles are often in conflict. Their objectives are different: one is therapy, while the other is forgiveness. Generally we do well not mix them up. I speak from considerable experience.

However, this separation of counseling from reconciliation does not mean that some elements of counseling techniques are not useful and helpful in the reconciliation rite. The priest uses whatever will help him secure the goals of effective reconciliation. He is, first and foremost, a reconciler using helpful counseling techniques and not a counselor using the rite of reconciliation to do counseling. As long as he keeps this distinction clear, he will not go wrong. The role of the priest in the sacrament of reconciliation is that of an effective reconciler.

Setting and Environment for Reconciliation. As much as possible, we should encourage each other to try the new rite "face to face." We all need to be encouraged away from "the box" and into the fresh light of the reconciliation room. I think that those in positions of church leadership have an obligation not to be neutral about the matter. The box is a bad sign.

Signs of the "box" are signs of alienation, not signs of reconciliation: the dark closet, the disembodied voice, the faceless presence, the mechanical sliding doors, no choice but to kneel. All these signs of the box are contrary to what the sacrament of reconciliation is all about. Our people need to know that these ugly signs came about for only one reason: to let the person hide and remain anonymous. We need to learn that these signs of alienation come to us from the most impoverished time in the history of the sacrament of reconciliation. It helps much if we are at least somewhat familiar with the history of this sacrament. It is almost impossible to talk intelligently about the new rite unless we know something of its history. We should be asking our homilists to be giving us more history rather than pep talks or moralizing sermons.

Parishes should provide inviting reconciliation rooms: lots of light, color, windows, plants, pleasant and comfortable furniture. No junk stuff. The arrangement of the room should invite a genuinely clear and free choice between the screen and "face to face." I have seen too many reconciliation rooms so arranged that the person who enters must deliberately choose to bypass the screen arrangement in order to make it to the open space. That is not a free choice. Adults do not deserve obstacle courses. Instead, the total environment of the room, as well as words and demeanor, should encourage people to the full experience of the reconciliation rite in the personal one-to-one encounter.

In addition, we do well to separate the rite of reconciliation from its unhappy association with Sunday Mass, confessions before Mass and the "Saturday afternoon and evening" syndrome. The separation of the two has already been started by many of the people themselves. The long lines that we remember are reduced considerably. The sacrament of reconciliation is not a weekend cleanup job. The sacrament should be available for people when they want it, for its own sake. Saturday should become simply one of the days when the sacrament is available.

Communal Celebration of Reconciliation. The future is going to be what we make it to be. The communal form of reconciliation is growing and being found acceptable. We are still working to develop the patterns. We have a considerable obligation to do it well, because these are the forms of celebration that bring us to the heart of reconciliation: reconciliation with one another, reconciliation with the community and, as a necessary consequence, reconciliation with self.

General Absolution: Good News, Bad News. The sacramental rite of reconciliation reaches its full dimension of life and power when celebrated as a community experience with general absolution. The rite for such a celebration already exists and has been experienced a sufficient number of times already. Most people who have tasted of it cannot say in words how much the experience meant to them.

Yet, at this writing, general use of the rite is not permitted. I cannot agree with this restriction and, along with many others, can only guess at the reason. There seems to be, on the part of those who exercise control, a fear that the experience of the full rite will deter people from seeking out the individual rite, from "going to confession" frequently. There could be other reasons: a desire to cling to the older, more restrictive theology of sacramental action or unwillingness to let theological renewal become widely experienced.

These fears are groundless. Things are actually working in just the opposite way. Those people who experience the full rite are the ones who are seeking the private "one-to-one" experience more often and more willingly! They have tasted and seen that the Lord is good. They want more. I do hope that the timid and fainthearted among our leaders will look at what is happening and listen to the voice of God's people. What is happening in the celebration of the full rite of reconciliation is all good news.

There is repentance in the land: many who were broken and hurt are being healed. Those who have gone away, who have been alienated by harsh practices, are wanting to come home again. In those places where people have been given the opportunity to experience this most complete form of community reconciliation, the church is beginning to shine as never before with the glow of the reconciling Jesus. It is important that we do not stop, that we do not turn back. We can feel it. Please, let us keep moving forward.

Celebrating within Present Limitations. In the meantime, while we wait not so patiently for the possibility of celebrating reconciliation in all its fullness or while we lobby to bring it about, let us celebrate the increasingly familiar rite of communal reconciliation with private confession in the best possible fashion.

The practice of communal reconciliation is current and growing. People seem to like it; they come in large numbers, at least in my experience. Some patterns of the community celebration of reconciliation are good, some are poor. Some patterns work and others do not. We are at a point now where we can, in view of our experiences with this form of the rite, clean up our act. I have some suggestions.

I should like to see the name "communal penance" disappear. It is not a good title. It gives out misleading vibrations. In that particular expression, we join the new word "communal" with the poorest word that we inherited from the old rite, "penance." The important word in this context is "reconciliation," even though it is a big word. Richard Gula put his finger exactly on the meaning of the word reconciliation in the title of his excellent book on the sacrament, *To Walk Together Again* (Paulist Press, 1983).

The Reconciling Community. The priest is the one who is empowered to give absolution in any sacramental rite of reconciliation. This does not mean, however, that he is the center or focus of a communal reconciliation rite: the community is center and focus. Reconciliation always takes place at the human level. We are reconciled to God because we are reconciled to our brothers and sisters. There is no reconciliation with God without reconciliation with brothers and sisters, just as there is no way of loving God without loving brothers and sisters.

In the early church community, the major signs of reconciliation were signs of being restored to the community. We have witness to that in the present order of Christian initiation (see *Rite of Christian Initiation of Adults*). If this entire process is done well, it is a work of the entire community. In those early days persons who had sinned seriously and publicly (murder, blasphemy, adultery) were put out of the community, usually for long years, and given hard penances. Their continuing relationship with the community, slight as it was, was guaranteed by the prayers the community offered for them. They were gone but not forgotten. When it was thought that they had repented enough, they were reconciled to the community by the bishop as the leader of the community, representing both the community and God.

Since that time, during the long dark years when reconciliation became totally private, the priest was seen as representative only of God, not of the community. And that is still the way that too many people see him today. So we need to be creating reconciliation services that put the focus back on the community. I have seen some experiments that have worked fairly well.

For the sake of creating a better life-giving symbol, it makes sense to hold such a service in a room where people can face each other rather than be confined to front-facing pews. If this kind of accommodation can be made in church, that is fine; but there is no reason that it needs to be held in church. What is important is that a beautiful environment be arranged to make the sign as effective as possible.

I have been present at services where different energies were being released in different ways: groups of people praying with each other and over each other. At the same time priest members and others were laying on hands. The ministering clergy were involved in all the action but not at the center of the action. In such experiences it comes through loud and clear that members of the community are really engaged in reconciling and healing themselves.

For some this might seem "far out." For others it is not. It is important to discover what the assembly is comfortable with. Many parishes are making delightful new discoveries through the process of thoughtful experimentation.

Including Individual Confession in Communal Celebration. Since general absolution is not officially available we need to talk about how we handle individual confessions during a communal celebration. Too often the major focus of the celebration seems to be, more than anything else, an excuse to get more people to go to individual confession. This is not the purpose of the rite. The purpose of the rite is to provide a community experience of reconciliation. To use the rite for the sake of individual confessions is a perversion of it.

How, then, do we work out ways of providing opportunity for private confession during or in connection with the communal celebration? The two do not really mix gracefully. We must realize that, no matter what we do, we have an awkward situation on our hands. But, through the process of parish experimentation, some creative patterns have emerged.

The most common pattern seems to be some variation of the following: If several priests are available, they stand at designated stations at the appropriate time. The community celebrants are instructed ahead of time to go to them, clasp hands if they so wish, offer a brief statement of their sins or sinfulness, receive absolution and return to their places. During this period the community engages in variations of silence, song and spoken prayer.

In another form the communal part of the rite is celebrated in its entirety. At the conclusion of the rite, ample opportunity is provided for individual confessions.

We have found also that having communal celebrations more often during the important liturgical seasons such as Advent and Lent makes a difference. When the services are more frequent, they are less crowded. More people have a chance to take part.

The custom is growing of not programming these celebrations "to take care of Christmas and Easter confessions." A number of parishes are gradually developing new expectations among their people. They are learning that the energy of the Triduum, for instance, is so demanding that provisions for reconciliation are not generally scheduled during Holy Week. People are learning to take advantage of all the reconciliation celebrations, communal and individual, during the weeks previous.

Parishes who hope to offer the best opportunities for the sacrament of reconciliation are programming both individual and communal forms often and at times that are convenient for the people.

All these forms are awkward attempts to substitute for the most desirable and the most workable form, the one that provides general absolution. But we carry on with these provisional forms in patience and good spirit while we wait for the full form to be released from captivity.

Encouraging Results. It is important that we do carry on with these communal forms because they are proving fruitful. People like them. People come in large numbers, gaining an altogether new but most essential experience of what reconciliation is all about. In greater numbers these people are abandoning the "laundry list" style of confessing. As a consequence they are beginning to come to grips with the issue of the real sins that play havoc in their lives and in the lives of others. It also has been noted that the more people experience the communal celebration, the more they tend to seek opportunity for the more leisurely one-to-one experience.

Most of all, people are beginning to perceive the more genuine image of a God who loves and loves and loves, and forgives and forgives and forgives. The experience of such forgiveness is really good news and creates a thirst for more.

No Time for Complacency. With a more inviting setting for celebration and a healthier and renewed understanding of the sacrament by priests and people alike, we still are faced with the fact that too many adults make childish confessions. How do we help adult people make adult confessions? My response is that if adults are helped to understand all that we have been talking about in these pages, they will themselves begin to deal with the demands of responsible adult Christian life. They will begin to discover their responsibilities to the community, to neighbor, to the poor, to the alienated. They will come to an awareness of their complicity in the major evils of society, such as the cancers of discrimination, racism and economic oppression. And they will want help and motivation for conversion.

As adults get to know themselves as a people sent out to proclaim good news, they get a chance to rise above their petty little private sins and begin to share some of the burdens of the universe, as Jesus did and as Jesus asks us to do. We have obligations to the present and future health and life of our communities.

The sacrament of reconciliation will become what we make of it. The guidelines are clear. Let's move into the future, helping each other get rid of the barriers that still hide the real promise of this sacrament.

We need to be sure that we are expressing the right theology of reconciliation when we put together the prayers, songs, readings and other elements of any given celebration. We need to be aware that the emphasis now is much more on God's mercy and forgiving love than upon our sinfulness and misery. The emphasis moves more toward acceptance and affirmation than toward guilt and punishment.

In our celebrations, both individual and communal, we need to hear the good news of God's forgiving love rather than the bad news of our sinfulness. We really don't need the bad news. We are filled with enough guilt and often are more depressed and discouraged than hopeful.

In many celebrations of the new rite that I have seen, I find that little has been done to update the language. The "examination of conscience" list is nothing more than a public form of the old "laundry list." The prayers are too often "me and God" prayers.

All of these elements of the celebration must be examined carefully to see that they express what the rite is all about. They need to be brought more in tune with the reality of God's love that we profess. Even while we are examining our sinfulness we need to know that we are bathed in God's love, and we need to make the signs that express it. Someday I hope to be part of a community celebration of reconciliation that is bathed in light and alive with confident song. I want to see the faces of my brothers and sisters and I want to shout out my joy. Please, let's not make a permanent pattern of dim shadows, flickering candlelight and sweet penitential music. Let's remember: we sin in the dark. We are forgiven in the light.

Signs of a Reconciling Community. If we are really serious about reconciliation within a given parish community we must ask the bottom-line question: what are the fruits? How can we tell that reconciliation is really taking place? It is one thing to celebrate the rite within a community and yet another for a community to be reconciled. The latter is the real goal of the reconciliation effort. It should be a declared goal, so that everybody knows what the expectations are and knows what fruits to look for.

How do you recognize a reconciling and reconciled community? How do you recognize a community that is struggling with the burden of peacemaking, even though the goal is not always achieved? What is the difference between this kind of community and one that is not doing anything at all?

By their fruits you will know them. First of all you will find more peace, and particularly more joy, whenever the community comes together. I'm *not* talking about the Pollyanna, huggy-bear, kissy-face superficialities we've all seen. I am not talking about just feeling good. It is quite OK to feel good. We need to feel good, but I am talking about conversion to a new way of life.

Inside the parish, I am talking about moving from self-centered to other-centered. I am talking about a parish community that gets serious about the business of making peace with one another and of serving one another. The fruits are these: fewer in-house feuds, less turf warfare, evidence of greater efforts at cooperation for the good of the parish, subordination of personal preferences for the common good, and greater acceptance of all kinds of different people, different cultures, different levels of wealth or poverty.

Outside the parish, I look for the expenditure of much more organized energy in what we used to call the "corporal works of mercy." A ministry that is experiencing conversion through eucharist and reconciliation puts out lots of energy taking care of those people outside the parish who need help. The list is long and demanding. We all know what it is.

If these signs do not show, we cannot claim that we are seriously and fruitfully celebrating communal reconciliation. We need to go back to the drawing board.

8

LIFE, DEATH AND RESURRECTION

We are bound to speculate about the mysteries of life, death and life hereafter. There is no way we can leave them alone. They touch our lives and destiny too closely. For that reason we also try to guide our speculation carefully and responsibly.

LIFE AFTER DEATH

Changes in the funeral rites, more than any other Vatican II changes, touched the lives of people immediately and deeply. This is true both because the changes were dramatic and because grieving about the death of anyone we love opens us to a depth of feeling we rarely experience at any other time. When we lose a dear one, we become vulnerable as never before. We are laid open equally to the pain of loss and to the love and care of other people. This is why the new funeral services can so easily and readily touch us.

No one could miss the drastic changes in the rites. Gone suddenly were the black trappings so long associated with death in the western world. Gone was the grim foreboding of many of the long-accepted funeral texts. The fearful imagery of the *Dies irae,* with its wrath and fire and the terror of a world breaking apart, gave way to the imagery of a new heaven and a new earth, a place of peace and serenity without sorrow or pain, a place where every tear shall be wiped away. The rite of absolution, a "purification" rite at the end of the funeral Mass and at the graveyard, became a "commitment" of the deceased not only to the tomb but into the hands of a loving God. Most of all we were called away from a morbid preoccupation with death to a bright and hopeful focus upon resurrection. What had been called a requiem Mass, a Mass for the dead, began to be called the "Mass of the Resurrection."

The change was mainly one of emphasis. The motif of new life was not altogether lacking in the former funeral rites, nor was the motif of hope absent. These motifs were present, but the overall emphasis was more on death than life. The fearsome imagery, partly because of timelessly powerful musical settings, overpowered the imagery of hope.

Even with the change of emphasis, the same powerful realities remain. Death is still a fearful separation and a deep mystery. We continue to feel the pain of loss. We continue to be cast down in grief. We continue to be afraid of our own dying. Fear of what comes after death still leaves us naked and vulnerable. Hell and purgatory still nag at us and still leave us unnerved and at the mercy of almost overwhelming guilt.

People want to know what lies behind this total "about-face" dramatized in the funeral liturgies. Is the church asking us to look differently at the mysteries of life, death and resurrection? Does the church know something we do not know? Is the church trying to share new insights with people? Is the church trying to give us a new theology of the four last things: death, purgatory, heaven, hell? People are asking these questions more than ever. And they have a right to ask.

The church has indeed come upon new insights, and these insights have the power to inspire a new quality of faith and hope for everyone. They are rich and satisfying; they are life giving.

It is the task of preachers, teachers and catechists within the church to open up these more recent insights gained from scripture and theology in language that people can understand. Theological jargon and esoteric imagery will not do. The leaders need to listen to the questions that are being asked and do their best to answer them.

Meanwhile we adults need to search out these insights as best we can. We need, most of all, to discover and share the new imagery so that we can think about these new insights and talk about them.

Here, as in other books of this series, we are dealing with *mystery.* We are dealing with mystery in its special and theological sense: no matter how many insights we have, we never get a clear answer. There is always more. God is not a problem to be solved, nor are we. We are mysteries that must be explored. This notion of *mystery* obviously differs from the popular use of the word in which clues are unraveled until there is a final solution.

The *mysteries* of which we speak are reality: a person, such as Jesus or a friend or oneself, or an event like death or life. A friend can be known to some degree, can be understood to some degree, but never entirely and completely. We can always go back for more. Isn't that, after all, the sheer delight of knowing and loving someone else? No matter how deeply we go, how much we discover, there's always more and more and more. That's why knowing and loving are such wonderful activities, such attractive activities. There's always more to delight and enchant. With God, of course, this goes on forever. And that's why heaven is forever. There is no end to God.

In the mysteries that cluster around death, resurrection and life hereafter, there are always some things we can know for sure. There are also those other things about which we can only speculate forever. Theologians and scripture scholars are constantly speculating about these events and coming up with new insights that lead us more deeply into the mystery. The human person cannot ever stop or be stopped from asking more and more questions and gaining more and more insights.

Most of the popular "knowledge" about death and resurrection is still the result of theological speculation in the past, particularly medieval theology. Our task in our time is to sort out from this speculation those insights that are persistently sure from those theories no longer valid because we have more historical information now than did earlier theologians. Thomas Aquinas and Duns Scotus and others, brilliant as they were, had definite limitations. They lacked the tools — original manuscripts, archeology, linguistic breakthroughs — to delve into the past and sort out fact from fancy, truth from speculation. Today we have these tools for reliable historical exploration.

Adults today have a right to know what we can say from clear evidence about death and life after death. They have a right to know which speculations about these mysteries can be advanced with confidence and which ones should rejected. They are legitimate questions.

It is no longer sufficient to tell adults that God will take care of everything. That is the old style of patting them on their heads like children and telling them they need not worry. We grownups are not so much worried as frustrated that our legitimate questions are brushed aside. It is high time for us as church to take these questions seriously and find out, as far as possible, what we can know for sure and what we can only speculate about. Adults are at their best when they know the limits of possible understanding. They know how to operate on those terms.

We are working with mysteries of faith, talking about matters that we hold true because they have been revealed to us through the experience of faith. Evidence for these realities comes from scripture and from the faith and worship life of the church. We are not working with scientific data, so we do not look for scientific evidence.

In these faith realities we want to be able to distinguish truth from speculation. The church holds as truth that Jesus was raised up, that he is in glory, that he possesses the fullness of the Spirit.

Yet we continue to speculate about what it *means* to be risen. What does it mean for Jesus? What does it mean for me? What does it mean to be glorified? What does it mean for Jesus? What does it mean for me?

Even within the area of speculation we distinguish between responsible speculation based on solid data and speculation that is not supported by such data. For instance, we know now that the apocalyptic imagery describing the end of the world is not to be taken literally. It is clearly an accepted literary form chosen to express important truths such as the continuing titanic struggle between goodness and the forces of evil, that Jesus prevails, that there will come an end to the struggle and that God's reign will come to its fullness.

Most of our speculation is worked out in images rather than ideas. For instance, what is the more valid image by which to picture the coming of Christ at the end of time? What image brings us closer to the reality of what Christ's coming is all about? I feel sure most of us imagine him coming to us from somewhere else in the same way we see the sun rising. But is this a really valid image? Does it tell us anything important about the coming of Christ that makes a difference in our faith life? So we question the image because it does not fit with the truth of Christ's presence in the world already. How can Christ "come" if he is already present fully in the whole world and all his people?

Such speculation drives us deeper into the mystery, forcing us to search for other images that more accurately represent the truths we are already sure of. As a result we get more deeply involved in the meaning of Christ's coming. As we get more involved, we begin to gain insights that have immediate and important consequences for our faith.

For instance, if Christ is already present in his whole world and in all his people, then his coming has to be imagined differently. More likely his coming will be an event that involves us and all creation. More likely his coming will take place in us and through us. More likely the coming of Christ involves the coming to fullness and perfection of all the energies of the universe, the coming to the fullness of human perfection of all his people. Such speculation is fruitful and life giving. It is the kind of speculation that brings grown-up people to deeper faith, renewed life and commitment. If grownups are denied this kind of healthy speculation, they are condemned to the fruitless and barren images of their childhood.

Faithful Christians believe that life after death is forever. They believe this firmly because Jesus said so. The revealed evidence for this truth is basically the word of Jesus and the evidence of his death and resurrection. Jesus did die. People saw him die. He was raised up and was recognized as the risen Lord by the same people who saw him die. They were convinced of this fact, unanimous and unwavering in their testimony. Jesus has passed from death to new life with God. He has made his own exodus journey and has returned to his Father. Jesus is with us for all time until the end, in and through the power of his Spirit. Jesus promised to send us his Spirit, the Spirit of God. All his disciples and the church hold fast to this truth and give constant testimony to it. Again and again the first disciples of Jesus experienced his presence in the power of the Spirit. The church has consistently given the same unchanging testimony.

Christians believe also that we all will die and will be raised up like Jesus. We have immediate and tangible evidence that we will indeed die. We see people dying. The evidence for being raised up rests on the promise of Jesus, upon the firm belief in the church from the beginning that we will be raised up and live forever. Jesus' promise rings out clearly, loudly. All who believe in him already have eternal life and will possess this life forever.

We believe also that we *already* are being raised up because the life that Jesus gives us right now — the life of *grace* — is a sharing in his own risen life. Resurrection actually is going on all the time. The process of being raised up is a process of being transformed. Like Jesus, and through the life of Jesus in the power of the Spirit, we are constantly being drawn from a life of bondage to a life of freedom. We are, like Jesus, passing over from the limits of life on earth to the total freedom of life with a loving God.

In the language of our biblical ancestors we are accustomed to calling that life of freedom the "reign of God." We speak of being on the way to the heavenly reign. We believe in God's rule. We believe that our destiny, the destiny of all people, is make it to God's reign and to be with God, with Jesus and with one another forever. This belief rests on a firm promise of God rooted in God's promise of covenant love: "I am your God, You are my people. I will save you." (Cf. Genesis 17:1–8) It rests on a firm promise of Jesus: "There are many rooms in my father's house. I will come and bring you there." (John 14:2–3)

But the image of God's reign immediately calls to mind a "space" and a "place." That image falls short of what it is all about. The entire notion of "God's reign" is God's unconditional love of all people. God's unconditional love for all people holds within it God's desire that all people will come together in a glorious life at the end of time. God wants to enjoy his chosen people and wants them to enjoy divine love forever and ever and ever. The image of "kingdom" is not able at all to convey this depth of promised life and love. We keep on struggling for images that will say it better.

We get closer to the real meaning of God's reign when we speak about it in terms of freedom and justice. God means for all of his people to gain as much freedom and justice as is possible in this life and, after death, their fullness.

In the Book of Exodus, which speaks of Israel's first encounter with God, God reveals himself as liberator. This revelation was acted out and confirmed by the events of the exodus journey. God said to Moses: "Go to my people. Tell Israel that I, the Lord, the God of their ancestors, the God of Abraham, Isaac and Jacob, have sent you to them . . . I will rescue you and set you free from your slavery to the Egyptians. I will save you. I will make you my own people and I will be your God." (Exodus 3) Through this revelation to Moses and through the experience of the exodus journey God revealed even more concretely his love and his plan. Through the exodus experience God made it clear that the destiny of God's people is freedom and that the way to that destiny is a journey of considerable difficulty, a journey of struggle and hardship, a journey of fear and uncertainty and great risk — a journey that demands a great deal of faith and trust in the God who loves us so much.

We persist in looking for the images that will help us get deeper into the mystery. Here is more. God created the universe and all people in it out of sheer love. God could have no other reason. Through the creative act itself God extended to all people their destiny to be fully human. But people can't do this by themselves. To become fully human we need more time than we have and more resources than we, as individuals, possess. In other words, we need God to be more and more present to us, more and more deeply a part of us, more completely a part of our lives and the lives of those around us.

We can still use the imagery of the heavenly reign here and hereafter, of God's reign over us, but we are releasing the image more and more from its space and time limitations. We do need God as "sovereign" and our lives to be lived in God's "sovereignty," "God's reign." We do need God alone to "rule" our minds and hearts, our whole being. We yearn for this kind of rule of God, this "being with" God and God's "being with" us.

Life, then, is certainly a journey. That is the best of all images. But it is not a journey from one place to another. It is a journey from human bondage to human freedom, from slavery to liberation, from reign to reign, from the rule of self-centeredness to the true rule of self-fulfillment with others in God.

It is no longer sufficient to tell adults that God will take care of everything. That is the old style of patting them on their heads like children and telling them they need not worry. We grownups are not so much worried as frustrated that our legitimate questions are brushed aside. It is high time for us as church to take these questions seriously and find out, as far as possible, what we can know for sure and what we can only speculate about.

In this deeper imaging of what the reign of God is all about, the role of Jesus becomes much clearer. Jesus is the new Moses. He comes not only to reveal God's love but to deliver God's people from the bondage of sin and evil in which they are caught so helplessly and hopelessly.

Jesus is leading us to the reign of God. He said so any number of times: "I am the way, the truth and the life. I have come that you may have life, the fullness of life. I am with you always until the end of time." (John 14:6ff.)

In the Gospel of John the message is clear that the one preoccupation of Jesus is to bring all people to this fullness of life, this unlimited freedom and peace. Jesus makes it clear that he was sent to do just that, and he makes it clear that he means to do just that. Jesus, who himself has gained this life of total freedom, is constantly about the business of leading all people, all creation for that matter, to the fullness of their destiny in this reign of God's life and love.

We also know and believe that this reign of God already exists on earth and is being brought gradually to its fullness. Jesus makes it clear that God's reign has already begun in him. The reign of God is at hand: we already are living the risen life of Jesus now on earth. Wherever people are working to bring about freedom and justice and peace in the world at any time, they are making the reign of God on the earth. That is what God's reign is here and now.

The church is part of God's reign but not the whole of it. The church of God and the reign of God are not the same. Just as Jesus was sent to carry out God's plan to bring all people to the heavenly reign, so Jesus in turn sent his disciples, his church, to carry out the same mission. The church is in the world as part of God's reign realized on earth. It has the task of witnessing God's plan for all people and of helping to bring that plan to life here and hereafter.

We know also that God's reign will come to its fullness. There will be an end to the rule of earth and we will enter forever into the rule of heaven. God has promised that there will be a "new heaven" and a "new earth." Jesus has promised that he will come at the end to bring to fullness and perfection forever God's reign begun in him. The Lord will come at the end: nothing is taught and held more firmly by the church. We know that the final coming of Jesus will mark an end and another beginning. It is a firm promise.

So if we add it all up at this point, we are sure of these truths: there is a reign of God and our destiny is to enter God's reign. The present world will somehow be transformed into a heavenly reign that will last forever. These revealed truths form a clear base for a strong and purposeful life. We know who we are, where we came from and where we are going. On the journey we have a powerful and trustworthy leader. That's a lot. We can depend on it and work with it.

There is a lot that we do *not* know about God's reign, about life after death. We have to speculate. We have to use our imaginations. This is often risky business. The imagination can fly off in all kinds of crazy directions, like some of the more far-out science fiction. But since we must speculate, it is better that we try to ground our flights of imagination in the reality that we know. There are different sets of clues that help us imagine what our life after death might be.

As previously mentioned, we do not take literally the scriptural descriptions of the end of the world. Scripture scholars show clearly that those images are a literary device, found in both the Hebrew and Christian Bibles, for speaking about the intervention of God in his world. The message is fact; but the imagery is a literary device.

At the same time, we can make some "estimations" about God's reign, estimations based on truths we already know. For instance, *where* is heaven? Is heaven *up there*? The fact that we think of heaven as a place can throw us off from the truth. It is almost impossible to imagine ourselves existing without existing in a *place.* There is no real evidence that heaven is a place. It may be, but we really do not know and we have no way of finding out.

We come closer to the possible reality when we speak of heaven as a "state" or experience. Heaven is promised as the fulfillment of all the good things we have ever known: joy, happiness, peace and justice for every person, without pain, evil or discrimination. Heaven, as an experience, promises all the best of what can make life on earth so humanly attractive. Relationship with others is the deepest and most valuable of all human experiences. The friendship and companionship of other people fulfills our deepest human longings. That is what heaven is going to be all about: love, friendship, companionship, hospitality, all at their full perfection, lacking nothing. These are indeed life-giving images.

It is not by accident at all, I think, that one of the persistent biblical images of life in the reign of God is the image of banquet. The banquet — being at table with friends, loved ones and invited guests — is rooted deeply in all cultures. Being at banquet means more than just eating. It means sharing in all kinds of ways. Whom I invite to my table and my hearth, I invite into my heart. This is precisely the promise of God's reign to every person: the companionship of God, of Jesus, of Mary, and the communion with all our sainted loved ones.

This image of banquet, this image of sharing and giving and receiving in active communion, is much closer to the possible reality of life in the reign of God than other static, less promising images. For instance, the notion of God on a throne with Jesus seated at his right hand should not be taken seriously. God never sits still. God is ever reaching out to us, looking for us, pursuing us. Life, energy, movement and companionship tell us the reality of the heavenly reign better than thrones.

Equally misleading is the image conjured up by the classical term "beatific vision," a working term of philosophers and theologians. It is a way of saying that face to face, immediate, full, joyful and complete personal presence is the kind of close and intimate relationship all people will have with God in the glorious heavenly reign. However, it is *not* an eternal sitting down and looking at God. As folk singer Ed Gutfreund put it:

> **"Will there be an intermission at the beatific vision,**
> **or will we have to sit and watch all day?"**
> — *Lights of the City*

No static image will ever help us envision the joy of life in God's reign.

There is another biblical image by which we are invited to understand what it means to live in the love of God. It is a sexual image. This sexual image persists in biblical literature and in the tradition of mystical theology. In the Bible the entire relationship of God with his people is described again and again in terms of the love between husband and wife. The tragic history of Israel is unfolded in the image of spousal fidelity and infidelity. It is as if God is saying to us, "If you really want to probe the heights and depths of our love together, you can find no more accurate image than sexual love and sexual fulfillment." The Song of Songs sings of the ecstatic rapture of the love of man and woman, giving us a glimpse of the fulfillment that awaits us in heaven.

When the great mystical theologians such as John of the Cross and Teresa of Avila tried to express the final rapture of the soul's union with God, they turned to the same imagery of sexual fulfillment. They could find no other image that would speak to the total possession by God of his loved ones, speak to the total self-giving of the lover to the beloved. The imagery is powerful, going into the heart of the reality of our union with God. It is powerful imagery full of live-giving energy. The tragedy is that we are not comfortable with such imagery. Such is the damage that Jansenist and Puritan heresies have wrought among us.

Another question that boggles our minds and imaginations is what we are going to be like in our own selves, in our own bodies, after death. Again, we can speculate in a number of ways. If we think of ourselves as made up of body and soul as two distinct parts, then we are going to envision two modes of existence after death: one from the time we die until the end of the world, and then another mode after the final coming when we get our bodies back again.

This kind of imagery is rather primitive and is based on a number of suppositions that I, for one, find difficult. It is based on the supposition that we really are made up of parts that can be separated. We have already discussed that theory of human dualism which tends to deny the essential and absolute unity of the human person. This view sees death as a breaking of the bond between soul and body. It allows the soul to continue on in the state of spirit until a later reunion with its body. The phenomenon of death as we perceive it certainly does suggest such an image. The person is dead: the animating principle we call soul no longer animates the body. The body eventually decomposes.

Human death, in its "natural" as well as violent forms, is convincing evidence for the body-soul image. Still, I find difficulties with this dualism. It violates the basic principle of the unity of each person. It forces foolish speculation, such as whether I will eventually regain my 20-year-old body or my 75-year-old body. Such crude imagery prevents further speculation that could lead to better conclusions. I am personally convinced that the unity of the human person comes first and remains an unchanging and unchangeable constant throughout any condition in which a person may exist.

Evidence for the unity of body and soul is strong. The consistent tradition of the resurrection in the church's teaching is strong testimony for the primary unity of the human person. Evidence that comes to us from the world of psychosomatic medicine is growing. Nothing happens in the body that does not also happen in the soul or psyche. All of this evidence supports the overwhelming conviction that human persons have their own indestructible unity.

In view of all this I am more comfortable with imagery that allows for some body-soul continuity throughout the entire process from birth through death and resurrection and the final coming of Christ. I prefer to hold to this hypothesis even though I have not too many clues for imagining how it takes place. But as scientists probe the mystery of the universe, their findings provide me with some glimmer of an idea. In the meantime I am willing to leave the logistics up to the Lord.

If we could know more about the present condition of Jesus in his risen life, we could get some clues about risen life for ourselves. But we don't know much. All we can do is speculate. We know that Jesus is completely himself as he always was. We know that he is free of time and space, transcending both. We know, therefore, that he is present everywhere, completely filling the whole universe. We know that he is glorified, but we do not know exactly what that means. From the evidence of revelation we can speculate that he has been completely transformed. He is Spirit-filled: he is in complete possession of the Spirit of God for all people. If we are going to be "like him in glory," we can imagine the same kind of transformation taking place in us to some degree: free persons transcending time and space, transformed like Jesus through the Spirit. We can imagine ourselves having it all together in a more wonderful way than we could ever dream of now. Such ways of thinking about what is to come can be far more exciting and inviting than the image that stops us cold at the graveside. We are called upon again and again by the prayer of the church to look forward with desire and longing to life hereafter with God. Therefore we need to present life after death in the kind of imagery that fits in with our own deepest needs and yearnings. I find adults becoming open to this kind of speculation. I find it has great meaning for them. It gets them past a blank wall, a dead end.

I think it is important that we keep on target in our attempts to imagine the coming of the Lord in fullness. It is somewhat naive to express the final coming of the Lord in apocalyptic images of a vast convocation of all the forces of the universe. The real meaning of the coming of Jesus has got to be expressed in terms of fulfillment, in terms of bringing to completion the full human capacity of persons, the full capacity of the universe itself. Jesus comes to us, in us and through us now. So why should it be different at the end? I've always liked Augustine's image: at the end there shall be one Christ loving himself. The imagery of Teilhard de Chardin appeals strongly to adults. They need such imagery in order to grow. They need to go beyond simplistic imaginings that are suitable only for young children.

ADULT SPECULATION ABOUT DYING

The act of dying is fascinating and fearful at the same time. Risk of the unknown always sets up vibrations of fear. When that unknown is so final and total as death our fears mount to a high level and reach such intensity that we simply do not face it. We ignore it as thoroughly as we can. We put it out of our minds and do not allow ourselves to deal with it. We yield only grudgingly to some consideration of our own dying when we are forced to encounter death in another person.

My personal fear of dying is very much tied up with my notion of God. If I think I am going to meet a stern judge and taskmaster, my guilt feelings can overwhelm me. If my chief way of understanding my face-to-face encounter with God is through the imagery of a searching examination, an evaluation followed by a cold, impassioned verdict, I am forced to be afraid. My fear becomes paralyzing when I think that, if I miss heaven and purgatory, I go to hell. Up to now, the general suggestion has been that heaven is hard to come by. In those cold and simplistic terms our situation seems grim.

I think that we can do a better job of imagining the encounter after death with a God who loves us beyond all telling. It is high time we took a closer look into the meaning of dying, of judgment, of purgatory and of hell. We need to talk about it with the adults of our community.

In talking about death with adults we need to come to terms with whatever is their own notion of God. Somehow we must begin to know and feel that through the act of dying we come fully and finally into the presence of someone who loves us dearly. It would be incredible, really, to think that someone who fully loves us all the time is suddenly going to become a stern and forbidding ogre. This kind of imagery is born out of notions of God that simply are not true. As we've said already, adults need the chance to look at all their false gods and destroy them.

Because of a long history of understandable misconception and irrational guilt feelings, the process of changing our image of God from stern judge to a truly loving person is difficult. Most of us do not succeed entirely, but with effort we can come well on the way. Our preaching about God and about what dying means should be calculated to help adults work their way out of this difficult and painful bind. We have been enslaved by fear for entirely too long.

We begin with the image of God and how we expect him to act when we are dying. I myself have come to expect that the one person who loves me more than anyone else is going to be right there with me at the moment when I need him most. I cannot think of God abandoning me at the moment I am most frightened and need him desperately. Even though my feelings do not always go along, I refuse any other image of God. When I think about dying, God has got to be there, keeping me and holding me in my last fierce struggle. I cannot conceive it otherwise. I don't want to conceive it otherwise.

I like what I have been reading about the act of dying in such theologians as Karl Rahner and Ladislas Boros. Their reflections on dying are supporting, life giving. Death is thought of as something I do rather than something done to me. Boros stresses that death offers a person the opportunity of making a first absolutely free personal act. Death for each person is that moment above all others for the awakening of consciousness, for freedom, for the encounter with God, for the final free decision about their eternal destiny.

In this view dying becomes the time for free decision such as no one ever had before. Everything is clear, as it has never been clear before. The full options and alternatives are exposed as never before. In this view of dying, there is no such thing as a sudden or "unprovided" death, even though the possibility of dying can still be sudden, even instantaneous. In the most recent speculation of theologians, the moment of dying is part of an ongoing process. It does not stand in isolation from the rest of my life. It is a moment that belongs to me as part of my life process, but it is also a moment the likes of which I've never had before. The momentum of my life does not carry me forward in a blind or relentless way: I can direct it and am responsible for it. In accepting the reality that dying will be part of my life, I can have an opportunity to look, to evaluate, to choose to be responsible. And I am not alone. I am held and helped by a loving God. The theologians are saying that the act of dying, no matter when and how it takes place, is the final moment in a lifelong process of free choosing. Such an image lifts my spirits and offers me much hope. It helps me cope with both guilt and fear.

So if we add it all up at this point, we are sure of these truths: there is a reign of God and our destiny is to enter God's reign. The present world will somehow be transformed into a heavenly reign that will last forever. These revealed truths form a clear base for a strong and purposeful life.

In this speculation the moment of death offers me a kind of stability that I cannot experience in life. It is a full encounter with myself as self, the likes of which I have never had before. It is in this notion of encounter with self that the business of final judgment finds its proper context. I see myself in the full light of God's love. I have, as never before, the opportunity for evaluating what I see: I pass a judgment upon myself. Dying is a definitive encounter with myself, just as it is a definitive encounter with God.

In this moment of judgment there is nothing arbitrary, whimsical or capricious. I am not going to be confronted suddenly with evidence that wipes out the accumulated evidence of my life. I will also have a freedom of choice in the context of total light. This means there will indeed be judgment: the very seeing of self in the clearest of all light is necessarily the act of judgment. Based on how I see myself, I make a choice. What are the options? The options have always been presented in neat and clear terms of a judgment issued by God for heaven, hell or purgatory. We need to examine our speculation about these things.

The church has always held for the three options of heaven, hell and purgatory. The church still holds them. What do these terms mean now? How are heaven and hell and purgatory to be imagined? We have already explored fresh possibilities for adult speculation about heaven as the fullness of God's reign.

The crudely primitive image of hell that we have inherited, a place of fire and brimstone to which people are condemned forever, contradicts belief in a loving and just God. A God who finally loses patience and gives up on any person is not God. An arbitrary and capricious God who would stop loving at the time of death is not the God of Jesus. Even under the civilized aphorism that the punishment should fit the crime, the crude traditional notion of hell does not hold.

The history of thought about sin and hell is full of absurdities. Even in the past few decades we had long lists of what were "mortal" sins and what were "venial" sins. The categories are sufficiently valid, but what we were told to put into them creates problems. To commit adultery, to miss Mass on Sunday, to fail to say the breviary on a given day have all been classed as mortal sins and as such deserving of the punishment of hell. Even the early church, it seems, held to three major "mortal" sins: murder, adultery and idolatry. To put murder and racial injustice in the same category as eating meat on Friday does not make sense to any mature, thoughtful person. It is an insult to God. No wonder most of us grew up with a warped sense of values. It took me forty years get things sorted out to make some kind of sense.

What is the serious possibility of hell as a final and irrevocable state of being separated from God? Is such a state possible at all? We have to raise the question because a lot of people simply do not think so. Let's take a look. When we talk of hell as an endless separation from God, we are talking about the real possibility of people becoming so engrossed in themselves that they are totally incapable of responding to God's love when that love is revealed in its fullness.

God does not condemn people to hell or to purgatory or to anything at all. People who condemn themselves to hell must be able, at any time but particularly at the moment of death, to see themselves clearly as they are and also see God in the fullness of his appealing love, and then coldly and deliberately walk away from that love forever. They must be so totally in love with themselves that God cannot get through at all. If people are capable of such choice, then hell is possible. Are there such people? Could anybody really make such a choice? When we look at the incredible love and mercy of God, his enduring and ever-forgiving love, it is hard to imagine that anyone would choose any other love but the love of God. When we come to understand the full meaning of the web of evil in which we all struggle, our pitiable weakness, the incredible emotional disorders to which we are prey, it becomes even more impossible to think that even the worst and most deliberately evil person is able to make the free choice of cutting self off from God's love. When that is possible, that's the hell of it.

To make such a choice is certainly possible. Not to able to so choose would mean that we are not free persons and not able to make free choices. Freedom of choice is an essential part of being human. A non-free human is a contradiction in terms. That is really not the problem. Our problem consists in trying to figure out how any human person goes about making such a drastic choice.

In the preceding speculations, I am not proposing definitive answers but, rather, possibilities. My point is that through preaching and teaching we need to help adults to undertake adult speculation about these mysteries. We need to help each other fight our way out of the guilt and hopelessness created by primitive and unexamined notions of sin and hell passed on as gospel truth. We must help people think about and work with imaginings about the afterlife which maintain as premises human freedom, human frailty and the total and unchanging love of God. The most important goal in helping people to think healthily about sin and death and hell is to help them be motivated to reach out in hope for the incredible love of God, not to beat them to death with fear.

The notion of purgatory, as we have inherited it, needs clarification as well. What is purgatory? Where is it? How long does it last? These are legitimate questions that thoughtful adults are asking. We have a serious pastoral responsibility to deal with these questions intelligently and thoughtfully. The notion of purgatory comes to us from an almost purely legalistic notion of God. We know that such a notion of God is alien to the God of Jesus.

Some theologian or other has said that the full-blown notion of purgatory is a triumph of thirteenth century canon law. It develops from the images of a prison sentence. It implies the image of a judge, a judgment and a legal punishment of a specific length. It implies an image of life after death as a linear extension of time, a time continuum that goes on at least until the "final judgment." It works on the assumption of two judgments, one immediately at the time of death and one at the end of time. This notion of purgatory is also mixed up with the medieval doctrines of merit and of indulgences. In that view, Christian living is pretty much the business of making and storing up points. And losing points. And the game goes on. It is intricate, complicated and totally unappealing. Gradually, though, we are learning to let go of this primitive reduction of God's love for his people to a point system.

Granted the validity of such things as temporal punishment due to sin, indulgences and prayers for the dead, we still need to free ourselves from the damaging fallout that comes from uncritical and unrestrained speculation on these realities. Says a contemporary theologian:

> "What has been defined about purgatory is quite minimal, something which must be kept in mind as we try to come to more contemporary language for it: 1) that purgatory exists as a state 2) where such temporal punishment from forgiven sin as still remains at the time of death is cleansed before admission of the dead person to the direct vision of God, and 3) these dead may be helped by the prayers and good works of those still alive."
>
> — Robert J. Schreiter, C.PP.S.
> "Purgatory: In Quest of an Image"
> (*Chicago Studies,* August 1985)

My own point, again, is simple: we are bound to speculate about the mysteries of life, death and life hereafter. There is no way we can leave them alone. They touch our lives and destiny too closely. For that reason we also try to guide our speculation carefully, responsibly. We hold suspect all simplistic images. We look for images that touch on the real issue. In the case of purgatory, the issue is purgation or cleansing or bringing to perfection — in other words, a continuation or completion of our life struggle, the struggle to grow up, to become fully and completely human.

Personal fulfillment is our destiny. God has called us to such fulfillment. That's what it means to live in God's reign. By ourselves, because of our selfishness and sinfulness, we are incapable of achieving our own fulfillment. For this reason God has already given us a share in his own life, his own power, to escape the bondage of our limitations and to gain perfection. We arrive at the moment of death with the job unfinished. There is more to be done.

It makes much more sense, therefore, to look at purgatory not so much as a time and a place but as the pain and anguish of that final moment of decision. In the blinding light of God's totally loving presence, we become painfully aware of ourselves as we are, still selfish and self-centered. Still closed up to God and to brothers and sisters. Still not fully open and free. Still not ready for the reign of God. So it happens that God, in his continuing love, completes in us what he began at the time of our birth. God makes us free. God brings us to the fullness of human perfection. God makes us full members of the heavenly reign. The process is painful and can be called purgatory. Such a view is a possibility. There are other, similar views. Such speculation leaves room for all that has been defined about purgatory.

This hypothesis of "final decision" also offers grounds for healthy speculation about babies who die. Babies, when they die, go to God directly and immediately. Babies, baptized or unbaptized, are born into a world that is already graced by God's love as well as struggling with the power of evil. Babies do not go to "limbo." Limbo is only a theory, an invention of twelfth- and thirteenth-century speculation. Medieval theologians were trying to make sense out of the same mysteries that we will always struggle with, and limbo was proposed as the destiny of the unbaptized baby who dies. Another logical question about babies who die is that it is hard to imagine an infant capable of living fully and completely in God's reign. It makes real sense, doesn't it, that infants also reach the fullness of human perfection at the hands of God. It is likely that no one is a "baby" in heaven!

What about our long-standing and beautiful custom of praying for our beloved dead? Does it make sense in this hypothesis of "final decision"? It is quite possible that they need our prayer to help in the final purification. Even if this or that person does not need our prayers, and we will never know that, I still think our prayers are a fine expression of good Christian piety. Since there is no before or after for God, only a continuing "now," there's no telling how our prayer for other people helps in the process of "final decision" or "final purgation."

Praying for the dead has additional value for us. Such prayer is a way we continue to remember those we have known and loved but from whom death separates us. This is our way of continuing to touch them with our love and also an expression of our being together in Christ. Our prayer expresses in a loving way our hope in Christ and our desire that all share in God's glorious reign. We don't give up this kind of praying easily, nor should we.

CONCLUSION

My purpose in this section has been to offer models for adult speculation and discussion of the "ultimate" questions. I have tried to show that speculation which emerges from asking the right questions can be fruitful and life giving. We have few answers. What we do have is the promise of God's reign and the assurance of God's steady love. All of us adults, precisely because as adults we are leaders, must help each other to wonder healthily about life, death and afterlife, not so much seeking "answers" as reaching out in new hope for the incredible love of God. If we are willing and able to pass on our soundly based speculation to the next generation, we are going to save them from a lot of the foolishness we had to work through as we struggled toward an adult faith.

PART 2

Talking
with Preachers
and Catechists

1
PROCLAMATION, ENTHUSIASM, PRESENCE

How should we preach and teach?

How should we talk with adults?

In short, preach it as if you mean it; preach it the way you feel it; preach it as if you believe it.

As preachers and teachers, we certainly must mean it and believe it and feel it. In reality that is a lot and also is not nearly enough. We have to make strong and clear *signs* that we *do* feel it and do believe it. What you see is what you get. Don't tell me; show me. People get the message through signs. They are not good at guessing. They should not be asked to guess, nor should they be kept guessing. Here, I am making a plea for that most wonderfully infectious human energy we call enthusiasm.

Will you start backing off at this point, with your stomach churning? Here we go again . . . more of that enthusiasm stuff! I hate it, you say, when someone gets too emotional. I can't take these characters who put on an act any more than you do. They turn me off too. I can't stand acts and I can't stand phonies.

When I say to preach what you mean, how you feel, how you believe, I am not at all talking about laying an ego trip on your people. When I say speak with enthusiasm, I am not suggesting that you "pour out your guts" and call that a homily. Save that kind of activity for your shrink; that's where it is appropriate.

However, I am saying that too much of our preaching is devoid of any enthusiasm whatsoever. Too often, turning your text over to a good lector would make a better impact.

If we were to isolate the most persistent general characteristic of Catholic priest preachers, we would have to say that their content is rational or conceptual. We preach mainly ideas and concepts, and we do it most correctly. Whether we are propounding the richness of Scripture or the teaching of the church or the ideas of even the best theologians, we are satisfied with being impassive messengers, representatives of authority. We preach like this: if you have problems with what I am informing you about, check it out with the sources. A show of conviction or enthusiasm is rare. I believe that the average white male preacher raised in the average Catholic seminary environment simply cannot overdo any feeling level. I have spent forty years working in seminaries. Year after year in my classes on celebration style, I dare my students to "over-do." I offer rewards. While I'm glad that some few do well, none of them have come near the possibility of claiming my offer.

I yearn to hear a preacher shout of God's love or tremble over the compassion of Jesus with the same amount of energy I've heard in preachers who inveigh against sin and tell people how they ought to be living. I want to see the true word of God get at least equal time with the senseless and unproductive moralizing that goes on.

Let me put it this way. I yearn to hear a preacher shout of God's love or tremble over the compassion of Jesus with the same amount of energy I've heard in preachers who inveigh against sin and tell people how they ought to be living. I want to see the true word of God get at least equal time with the senseless and unproductive moralizing that goes on.

As the most general context for how we *should* preach, I refer

144

again to Joseph Gelineau's thought in the very first pages of this book. The primary function of the homily is prophecy in the New Testament understanding of the word. This prophecy is the proclamation of God's coming into our lives through Jesus right now. What we must preach is what we know and feel and believe is happening right now. All preaching in the context of celebration is proclamation and invitation seeking a response right now. Preaching is all about something happening here and now.

Through sacramental celebration we claim that Jesus works his saving love in us in this present moment just as really as he ever did in history. He could not have been more really present to any other people at any time than he is right now. In fact, Jesus in the power of the Spirit is more really present to us now than he was in his ministry on earth centuries ago. He is closer to us now; we are closer to him now than were his friends before the resurrection.

That breathtaking truth is what we need to know and feel when we are preaching as part of sacramental celebration. It is all going on right now. Preachers need to be intoxicated with this insight. If they cannot find this truth from their own experience and education or from our discussions here, then they must find it somewhere. If this is not the beginning energy of preaching, how can people ever get to experience such a wonder?

It's said that what is most important in education is what is "caught" rather than what is taught. In no circumstance is this more true than in the moment of life-giving preaching.

Preaching that is genuinely proclamation is not different than the proclamation style that marks a life-giving reading of the word. Preaching does not "take off" from the reading as from a launching pad. Effective preaching is a full continuation of the word; it is a further breaking of the word in the same way you break bread. The preacher has the task of helping people in those moments to get more deeply involved with the word that has been proclaimed. If the preacher breaks it, tastes and savors it, people have a better chance to do the same. In this very human way, the preacher begins to unleash the power of the word. He is helping to release the power of the Spirit of Jesus in this particular parish at this particular Mass.

God's word has never been heard except in human accents. The power of God's word is limited or enhanced by the quality of the human word. A dull, listless reading of the gospel is just as boring as a dull and listless reading of the phone book. A quite correct but lifeless preacher turns people off as much as any lifeless lecture anywhere at any time. These facts of communication are as universal and inexorable as the law of gravity.

A preacher who knows his job realizes very clearly that he is not teaching a lesson. He is not an instructor lecturing in a classroom. If he really knows his job, he is seeking to bring about in the lives of people an "experience" of God's word. He knows that any "experience" of the word will take place within the frame of what we know as the experiences of people. He knows that if he can help create the wonderful human experience of persons sharing the living word, the living word will burst forth. He knows that the most valuable kind of learning is taking place in the experience, learning that goes deep and lasts long. All this can happen precisely to the degree that he does not become a self-styled teacher and to the degree that his style is not deliberately didactic. I think this is true for catechists as well.

The most important part of life-giving preaching is the reading itself. The reading must be life-giving. We need to do something about how readers proclaim Scripture. We need to be honest and say that few readers proclaim anything. They read correctly, but they do not proclaim in a life-giving fashion. Most of the reading of the scripture at parish masses on Sunday is dull and complacent. It is spiritless. It bores people to death.

We ask people to put down their books and listen to the readers. Why should they? Nothing important is happening, so why bother? When we let poor, dull, inadequate, incompetent reading go on Sunday after Sunday, we are saying loud and strong for all to hear that it just isn't important. We are saying to all our people that mediocre is OK, that sloppy is OK. We never tolerate on radio or TV or in the movies the kind of uninspired reading nourished in our churches Sunday after Sunday.

Do something about this problem. We've been tolerating destruction of the word for too long now. We need to stop wistfully talking about having better reading and start doing something decisive about it.

The most important part of life-giving preaching is the reading itself.

Much needs to be said about reading skills. I've had a go at it in the book *Proclaiming God's Love in Word and Deed*. In the selection on readers and also presiders, there are simple, immediately workable suggestions for improving the proclamation of Sunday reading. What you find there applies to all readers, including priest-readers of the gospel.

In brief, I say that readers need to look up, look alive, look alert, look at people, tell the story like it is. Tell the story with credible excitement, showing that you want other people to get excited about it. Stand tall, look tall, feel tall and proclaim the word of the Lord! Strike for the person sleeping in the back pew. Bother him or her. They might begin to listen. That's all the Spirit needs. I would offer the same advice to preachers.

Any preacher who communicates how he feels about the gospel is bound to reveal something of self. And that's exactly how it must be. The very first principle of all ministry is to give of yourself. Ministry is not doing things for people, laying a service on them from the outside. That is what hired hands do. This principle of self-giving prevails in all ministry. Presiders give of themselves through their signs of celebration and proclamation. Readers give of themselves in their own signs of proclamation.

Music ministers give of themselves through the music signs they proclaim. It is the sign that counts, not the intention. What you see and hear is what you get.

For the preacher at Sunday Mass this principle of revealing self is very important. He gets lots of prime time whether he deserves it or not. The preacher has a captive audience which he can bore to death or bring to life. As a music minister, I have had to scrape many a celebration off the floor after a preacher has left it there wounded, quivering, dying, sometimes dead. It really is not fair. A person with so much power over life and death needs to be sensitive to his or her power and not abuse it.

There are two self-images that help a preacher move more easily in the task of communicating self. In the first, see yourself not as communicating ideas but as thinking and feeling your way through what you have prepared. Focus on the people gathered rather than on the ideas, and try to relate directly and immediately with the people. Don't eyeball them to death, but don't hide behind ideas and words either. Since preaching is speaking and hearing a word, it helps no end when the community is responsive. Personally, I'd buy dinner for the first person who smiles or nods affirmatively or encouragingly to me when I preach.

The other self-image is that of searching and learning and growing with the people in the same moment that you are sharing the word with them. In order to do this, you must be able to see yourself first as a member of the community before you see yourself as leader of the community. Accept the simple truth that you live under the judgment of the gospel like all brothers and sisters. Know that you must grow in faith and in hope and in love. Know that if you express your own faith you will help your people grow in their faith. Know also that as they respond to you, and as you let them in, they are strengthening and deepening your own faith. Know that faith grows and flourishes in the moment of sharing. Invite the Spirit to be free to lead you on.

How many times have I suddenly heard the words of the gospel I am reading as if I had never heard them before! I have also learned never to prepare my homily notes so tightly that there are no open spaces. I deliberately leave spaces now because I have discovered that the Spirit practically always has something better to say. So much for the "how" of preaching in terms of style: proclamation, enthusiasm, presence.

2
FOUR CONTEXTS OF GOSPEL PREACHING

The next question: how do you, the one who preaches, come by the word you are preaching? How do you search out the texts and uncover the themes you are opening up for the faith of your people? So far, I have tried to offer some possibilities for discovering and preaching major Bible themes. I asked two questions: what does the church need to know about the good news in order to become church? What do adults need to know about the good news in order to live adult Christian lives? Then I proceeded to touch on some major themes and to develop them to some beginning degree. The principle underlying this procedure is that very often, when you go to the Bible, you do not find what you should find until you know to some degree what you are looking for. I hope the following approach is helpful to you.

I have developed a procedure for getting at Bible texts from Sunday to Sunday, a procedure which helps uncover the basic themes we have been talking about. I call it "getting at the text through context." The principle goes like this: Any given reading for any given Sunday is never an isolated reading. It belongs within a context, several contexts actually. While some selections are easier and more self-evident than others, no scripture excerpt can really yield its depth of meaning unless it is seen and understood within its series of natural contexts. I identify four contexts and will review them briefly. In summary, these contexts are:

1. Good news itself
2. Liturgical seasons
3. Specific texts chosen for reading
4. Immediate situation of the human community

Before exploring the flow of homily preparation through these four levels of context, let's review what a homily is supposed to be according to the Constitution on the Liturgy. The style of preaching that prevailed before Vatican II was different from the style urged upon us now. Even though the homily, in contrast to the sermon, was actually catching on before the council, the prevailing style was different. Basically, we "used" isolated segments or verses from scripture to give "authority" to whatever we chose to talk about. Usually, the readings of the day supplied most of what we needed for this purpose. We used verses which "fit," which helped make our point. I am not making an indictment. I am simply describing the reality of the kind of preaching, good and bad, that we grew up with.

One of the driving forces behind the reform of the sacramental rites as set forth in the Constitution on the Sacred Liturgy was an attempt to restore the word of God to its rightful place in all sacramental action, particularly Sunday Mass. It was very clear to the fathers of the council that the word had been lost almost altogether. Out of this purpose came the new lectionary with its fuller exposure of the word of God over a period of three years. Out of this driving purpose of the council come our guidelines for preaching today. The purpose of the homily is to open up the Bible, God's word, so that people are able to hear it, understand it, respond to it and gradually be transformed by it. It is practically impossible to fulfill this mandate for preaching unless we work hard to establish the context for the Sunday readings.

By background and preparation the priest-celebrant is supposed to be better equipped than others to discover and establish this altogether necessary context. The task of giving the homily, the responsibility for opening up God's word for the people, has been reserved for the priest or deacon out of the unexpressed assumption that he is more qualified than others to do so. Through his years of seminary study he has been exposed to the theological and scriptural tradition of the church. He is supposed to have made a great deal of this tradition his own so that it influences his way of thinking and feeling and acting. Because of his background he is supposed to be able to search out the proper and necessary context for the readings apportioned for each Sunday's celebration. A paragraph lifted from the Old Testament is simply a paragraph from the Old Testament, nothing more. The same paragraph opening up the good news is something else. The preacher is supposed to supply context. Sometimes he does; too often he does not. We have to guess whether it's because he doesn't know how or because he was too lazy to do the job. In any event, context is what he is expected to make.

THE FIRST CONTEXT: GOOD NEWS

The largest context of any Sunday homily is what is called *kerygma* in schools and treatises. *Kerygma* is the Greek word for the good news itself in contrast to *didache* which is the teaching about the kerygma that has accumulated through the centuries. We have no need to propagate this technical language once we understand it. In simple language, the first context is the core message of salvation, the good news itself, God's plan to summon all people to the Kingdom through Jesus Christ. This core message has many expressions, but it would seem that any valid statement of it must contain certain basic elements. I myself put these elements together in the following manner:

God loves you totally all the time
without reservation, without restriction,
whether you are good or bad or indifferent.

You cannot win or lose God's love.
God wants you to accept his love
and to love him and your brothers and sisters in return.
That's all. No price or payment, no conditions.

Jesus is God's gift to you,
to show you and tell you how much God loves you,
to gather you together and bring you back to him
through the only way possible, the way Jesus went back
to God, through his dying and rising.

Jesus is risen and he is with us.
Jesus is present in the whole universe, in all people,
working in the power of the Spirit to bring all people
to the Kingdom. Jesus is present in his Church
as in his body on earth, in his community of disciples
who are called to proclaim his saving action
and to be a visible and life-giving sign
of his reconciling love.

I participated recently with a group of people who were responding to the 1979 FDLC document *Discovering the Good News in Our Midst.* One of the chores was to formulate the Christian gospel in some sentences. Following is my own more recent try at formulating the core of the gospel message.

God's faithful covenant love is for all people
without exception or reservation.
God's covenant love binds us, at one and the same time,
in love to God and to all our sisters and brothers.

God's plan for all people is that they "pass over to
the Kingdom" by way of love of neighbor. God's plan,
as revealed by the Spirit of Jesus through creation,
is the center and focus of all biblical revelation.
The mission of Jesus is to show God's love to all people,

153

*to gather them together and to bring them back
to the Kingdom.*

*Jesus carried out his mission through his self-giving
in his own life, death and resurrection.
The same mission of Jesus, who is alive and with us
to the end of the ages, is carried out now through all people,
and in particular by the church,
charged by Jesus to go out and proclaim the good news.*

In both of these statements I have tried to touch on all the important elements of the good news. Perhaps you would prefer something even as simple as this:

*God loves us, all the time.
Jesus is risen and is with us until the end of time,
bringing God's saving love in the power of the Spirit.*

In any case, I think you see what I mean. Always keep the core message before you, so that you can figure how the reading at hand derives from the core message and expresses some part of it. I suggest that you make up your own statement of the gospel message so that you have it at hand all the time. The core message never changes. You can say it to children, you can say it to adults. The language may change as often as you wish; the message does not change.

Some Sunday, ask the people at Mass to have a try at forming their own statements of the good news during the following week. Give them some idea of what you are looking for; ask them to turn them in, if you want, and then carry on some follow-up. Or ask them to do some homework during the week, and you will share with them your own effort the following Sunday. Things like this can help people begin to really understand what we mean by "good news."

To summarize: without the primary context of the good news,

your preaching is doomed to wander in circles, coming from nowhere, with no place to go.

THE SECOND CONTEXT: LITURGICAL SEASONS

A second very valuable context for understanding the scripture readings from Sunday to Sunday is provided by the church in the calendar of liturgical seasons. This context developed quite naturally from beginnings in the early church. It developed because humans are creatures of time and space, and they need time and space in order to take hold of any great truth or reality and make it their own. The central reality of God, the total other, the transcendent one, cannot be grasped by people except partially and in time sequences. It is the same for the overwhelming reality of the risen Jesus, beyond time and space, blinding like the sun in all his glory.

Out of the catechumenate practice came the period we now call Lent. This period was for renewal of the whole community as well as for final preparation of the catechumens.

The sun is a good example of how it all works. The sun, in a true sense, is made for eyes, and eyes are made for the sun. Our sun is the source of all light and eyes are for seeing in the light. But if the naked eye gazes at the naked sun even for moments, it not only cannot see but becomes overwhelmed and blinded by the very source of its light. So we experience the limitless energy and light of the sun only during part of each day, and only indirectly.

So it is with the church seasons. We put time up against the timeless reality of God and Jesus, and we adjust the reality to our capacity to receive it. At the beginning of apostolic times, there was just Sunday, the Lord's Day, "little Easter," on which was celebrated the single total reality of Jesus dying and rising.

Also, of course, there was the anniversary celebration of Easter, the great vigil — no Holy Thursday, no Good Friday, just the Easter vigil celebration. During the fourth century came the beginnings of separation: Friday for commemorating the death of Jesus, Saturday and Sunday for celebrating the resurrection. Then came the beginnings of celebrating the Last Supper on Thursday. That development led to the "sacred triduum" which we still celebrate.

During these centuries another time period was developing. Out of the catechumenate practice came the period we now call Lent. This period was for renewal of the whole community as well as for final preparation of the catechumens. The time after Easter, when the community continued to gather with the new members to deepen their understanding of the meaning of the very wonderful experience they just had, resulted in what we call the Easter Season. The Lent and Easter seasons give us the time, recurring time, to absorb the great timeless mystery of God and Jesus.

Later on, through further historical development, there came the other seasons of Advent, Christmas, Epiphany and the long succession of "ordinary" Sundays. Also came saints, saints and more saints, all those Christian heroes who were held up for us as examples. As the number of feasts and seasons grew, and rogation days, mini-seasons and many feasts of Mary were added, the liturgical year became complex and jumbled. That is why Vatican II called for and got a reform of the whole liturgical year. Now the seasons shine out clearly for all of us, with their meanings restored. Much of the clutter has been removed: the saints, so to speak, have been put in their proper place, and the major feasts of Jesus' death and resurrection shine brightly again on the yearly horizon.

In and through each of these seasons, particularly the major ones of Lent and Easter and Advent, the church celebrates the same reality: the dying and rising of Jesus. But each season gives a different shape and color and nuance to the reality, so that we are able to celebrate fruitfully and with a fresh approach. I always thought that was pretty smart of the church. Just when we can't stand another Easter song, it all changes. We get a new start or some quiet time as on the ordinary Sundays of the year.

Each of these seasons gives a context to the readings that have been carefully chosen for use during that time. This second context, if we understand it and follow its lead, provides most of the focus and content for "thematic" planning of Sunday Mass celebrations. In the seasons of the church year we find the natural themes for Sunday celebration. These themes are not forced or twisted. They arise easily out of the focus of the season, which is always set on the core proclamation of the good news.

If we stay with the seasonal focus and the seasonal meaning, we avoid what seems to be a growing passion for making up what I would call artificial themes for Sunday celebration. There is no easier way to lose focus and perspective of the good news. When we start stuffing Sunday into "themes" instead of "discovering" the themes as they are expressed in the readings already carefully chosen, we are in trouble. Whim and caprice begin to be the arbiters of Sunday celebration rather than the good news of God's loving plan. Some excellent materials are available to help us "get into" the seasonal themes of the church. We ought to search them out and get our preachers and planners to use them.

Please note the progress you are making. Work the particular Sunday texts back into the core message and see what part of that message they bear. You are already getting light on the particular text. You know more about it, how to understand it and talk about it. Then, as you absorb the color of the season in and through the same text, you uncover further layers of meaning. In light of the season the text reveals more meaning, yields further understanding of the mysteries it represents. The process is exciting and interesting. The well never seems to run dry.

There are two points to note here. First, there's the question of how to deal with the constant intrusion of all kinds of "special" Sundays: mission appeals, diocesan appeals, bishops' letters, Mother's Day, Father's Day, national holidays and so forth. The list is endless and if you are undisciplined about it you are licked forever. You will never get any momentum in any direction at all. In this matter you have to be strong and firm. You have to manage all these "specials" and keep them in the perspective of your unwavering purpose to preach always the good news first. To the extent that you permit other special occasions to wreck your program, you are responsible for all the bad news they engender. You must have ingenuity and firmness of purpose to fit them into place. I know this much: People who are determined about this do find ways that work.

The second thing worth mentioning is more of a wish, but it needs to be said. The restored lectionary is a good piece of work. The main task mandated by the Constitution on the Sacred Liturgy has been done, and the word restored to its rightful place in Sunday celebration. After several years of experience with the three-year cycle of the readings, some of us regret that the arrangers of the lectionary have not given us a three-year cycle of only the clearest and strongest Bible readings that bear the core message of the good news. If there were perhaps only one reading each Sunday, we would be spared the difficulties of having to ferret out the more pertinent parts of the message from some of the more obscure readings. In a sense, this is exactly why I started thinking of the need for a book such as this. I have observed the regular phenomenon of priests preaching the new lectionary without ever getting around to the core message. All too often they wind up preaching peripheral stuff, yielding too easily to the temptation of picking and choosing until they find something that suits their personal fancy or preoccupation. The good news doesn't get heard too often.

THE THIRD CONTEXT: SCRIPTURE READING

There are a lot of questions we need to ask about the text chosen for readings. We have already asked some of them: What is the relationship of this text to the core message? What is actually being proclaimed? Before we decide what we think the text is saying, we need to do the homework of finding out, as best we can, what the text is actually saying. For this task, we need the help of reliable Scripture resources commonly available to us all.

It might help if I gave an example of the kinds of insights you get if you work carefully at this level. Take the parable of the owner of the vineyard hiring workers to go into his vineyard at different times during the day and then paying them all the same wage at the end of the day. When the workers complain, he tells them to mind their own business. He will do it his way. His way is different from human ways. A second meaning is that this parable was the response of Jesus to complaints that he was paying more attention to sinners, tax collectors and whores than to the establishment. His response was that he will do it his way.

The early church, the church that wrote the gospels, recalled this parable of Jesus at when they were accused of paying more attention to the gentiles than to the Jewish members of the church. Again, the response was: God's ways and our ways are different. Learn from us if you can, but don't try to impose your narrow, selfish standards on God's unlimited love.

With this kind of historical background we can begin to figure out how we might understand this particular parable and talk about it in our parish, in our particular neighborhood, in our particular year of the Lord. The parable tells us a lot about the kind of God we have, about his love and care and justice for all. The parable certainly can help us measure our behavior here and now in the clear light of the good news; it can help us face how exclusive we are in our church society, how we run it often like a country club.

What about the large variety of homily helps that clamor for clerical attention week after week? I have one single concern about these resources. Too many preachers do not know how to use homily aids. Too often the materials in the published homily services are passed from preacher to hearer without going through the head and heart of either. If you find a good homily help and know how to use it, fine; but be sure it is not using you!

When you stand up on Sunday to share the life-giving gospel of Jesus with your people, his people, you are standing in the presence of people at every conceivable level of faith and hope and love. You are celebrating with loving peacemakers, kind and compassionate lovers who are already giving their lives in service of brothers and sisters.

You become a good preacher only if you grow through your own efforts to wrestle with the Bible. If you are not willing to wrestle with your own discovery of the message, if you are not willing to do your own homework, you will not become the kind of preacher who can speak with faith and conviction about the good news of Jesus. To be an effective preacher, you just have to communicate your own self, your own faith in the signs you make in your preaching. If you have no self to communicate, no struggling faith to share, then you really should not preach at all. Preaching is proclamation and celebration. The energy of celebration is personal presence, the giving of self, the "sharing" of the good news.

We have seen that the essential contexts for preparing to preach are the core message of the good news, the human time frame we call the liturgical year, and a willingness to explore the biblical text itself. However, if the homily is indeed to be the proclamation of a present fact and present event by you, who are moved and excited by this event, to human persons who should also be moved, then one important additional context is needed.

THE FOURTH CONTEXT: IMMEDIATE HUMAN SITUATION

Jesus has to be incarnate in those people to whom you are preaching on this very Sunday. Jesus has to belong to these people here and now. He needs a recognizable face. He needs to become real. People have to be able to think and feel that they can be in touch with him. These people here and now need to know that what Jesus says can make all the difference in their efforts to get meaning into their lives and into their struggle to survive. They need to know that Jesus is present, helping them to make it from day to day, week to week, year to year.

When you stand up on Sunday to share the life-giving gospel of Jesus with your people, his people, you are standing in the presence of people at every conceivable level of faith and hope and love. You are celebrating with loving peacemakers, kind and compassionate lovers who are already giving their lives in service of brothers and sisters. You are looking at people filled with the wonder and excitement of fresh young love. You are beholding people shining with the marvel of old, experienced love and tenderness. You are facing wealthy people and poor people, the well-off and the cast-off. You are looking at people infected with the disease of racism: both the afflicted and the afflicting. It makes little difference whether they are black or yellow or white or brown or any mixture in between. They are there, and they are hurting. There are people before you who are struggling with the oppression of the institutional church. There are fearful people who had once found security in the old church and old politics; all that was real and true for them has vanished. They feel that they have been wiped out, and nobody really cares.

You have all these differences and many others. But you will know in the same moment that all the people, whoever they are and at whatever level, *all* are touched by the irrational uncertainty of life and sickness and suffering and dying, the pain of separation, loss, rejection, loneliness and alienation. You will know that, mixed in with all this pain, you can count on bright faith and love to be shared by all, with all.

This is an most important context for preaching and celebrating. It is the one we most neglect. We need to make a serious and consistent effort to know it, to be pastorally sensitive. The gospel must be preached to all these people who have come. The gospel has something to say to each one and to all. If we try, and keep on trying, the Spirit of the healing Lord will help us to express what is good and valuable for all, and not to make too many mistakes as we go. Count on it.

But please do your homework. Get to know your people. Avoid, as much as possible, the stereotype. Focusing on stereotypes is worse than just simply not knowing. Above all, listen. Listening keeps you from getting out of touch. A sensitively pastoral person will make every opportunity listen to people and take seriously what they say.

There are several levels of listening. The most important level is letting people tell their own story. Let them tell you who they are and where they are coming from and how they feel about themselves and about the parish and about what's going on around them. Don't make judgments; don't attempt to "correct" what may seem to be an unenlightened or prejudiced judgment. Just listen. Take it in. Listen carefully so that, as much as possible, you *hear* what is being said. One of the best signs you can make, that will make good listening a possibility somewhere down the line, is the practice of standing outside the church building to greet your people before Mass begins. They will begin to trust you and they themselves will begin to listen to you.

The separation between people and clergy that began over a thousand years ago has not been healed enough. It persists like a stubborn disease. Clericalism still remains the greatest single cause of alienation in the church. The artificial "clerical world" begins in the seminaries and continues through life with separate thought patterns, feeling patterns, ways of life, values and institutional structures. The pity and tragedy is that we don't seem to realize the situation.

I am most pointedly concerned here about the fact that the existence of the two "worlds" makes communication very difficult. On Sundays there are two important dynamics going on: someone is talking and others are listening. There is no guarantee at all that what is being said is being heard. People really listen only when they can identify in some way with the person who is talking. If people cannot make this identification and if you, the preacher, do not make an effort to identify, there is little or no communication. This identification is the absolutely essential base of any trust or credibility. If people cannot identify with you, they cannot trust. That is the sad state of affairs in too many churches on Sunday throughout our land.

3
LANGUAGE

The *language* of today's preaching needs much attention. A homily is not an essay, not an exegesis, not a theological tract. A homily is "familiar conversation" with people who understand and appreciate plain English. All of us who have done specialized work in theology or scripture pick up the professional jargon, often without realizing how much. We tend to preach that same jargon. We do not realize how little we are communicating. Let's face it: professional language does not communicate beyond the classroom. You can give a great sermon and people will admire you to some extent, but they will not have a clue as to what you are talking about. They won't tell you this, either. They will grin and bear it and admire and pretend they understand.

So the first thing you do is get rid of the jargon. Do it deliberately, ruthlessly, insistently. It is pathetic to hear preachers Sunday after Sunday talk about the celebration of "these mysteries," the "paschal mystery." Even the word "liturgy" is jargon. "Sunday Mass" still communicates more to the average person than does "eucharistic liturgy." Another one is "eternal life"; this one is used as if it meant something that comes after you die, if you are lucky. We know, or should know, that the gospel meaning of "eternal life" means life right now, the risen life of Jesus in the power of the Spirit. Some younger preachers still try to lay Greek words from their seminary classes on their listeners. These are just a few examples. Sometime, very soon, alone or with others, brainstorm your working vocabulary and check it out for jargon. You will be amazed at how much of it you use without realizing how few of these words have any meaning for most people.

At the risk of upsetting some, I would like to suggest that many of the translations of the sacramentary prayers offend in this area. Even the concepts that are expressed in the prayers do not mean very much to the people who are supposed to identify with the prayers and make the prayers their own. One outstanding example is the constant "put-down" of "this life" in contrast to life hereafter. People do not even listen to this stuff anymore. Their intuitions and hopes are well beyond the kind of paternalistic advice expressed in these prayers. Some of the alternatives offered for the opening prayer at Sunday Mass are OK, but too many of them are verbal overkill. We are willing to be patient and understanding for a while about the process of creating suitable official prayer. But only for a while. Much work needs to be done, and fast.

So the first thing you do is get rid of the jargon. Do it deliberately, ruthlessly, insistently.

We give credit to the International Commission on English in the Liturgy (ICEL) for giving us a beginning. We understand the practically impossible guidelines under which they operate, since there are many diverse English-language cultures. Thanks for a good beginning, ICEL, but please help break the mold. Help us to get on with the process of making our own prayers in our own speaking language. Don't be satisfied with anything less. Remember that the church in these United States of America is not altogether upper middle class white. Much of our genuine vernacular comes from the Anglo-Saxon roots of our culture, not from our Latin and Greek humanistic background.

Most of us who preach come from a background of classical humanist education. We have been immersed in it and have soaked up much of its influence. We are not aware, I am sure, of how many long words we use, words of many syllables, words that come from our Latin and Greek background. (I was going to say how many elongated, polysyllabic Latinate words we use, but I gave that up in favor of the vernacular.) The Anglo-Saxon part of our language inheritance offers many more short, to-the-point words that bring meaning faster and more surely than their Latin cousins. Remember that we curse in Anglo-Saxon and nobody misses our meaning.

Preachers will profit from the following discipline. Each week, sit down after you have worked out your preaching for the coming Sunday and write out a short, carefully phrased statement of the theme, such as you would offer at the beginning of Mass. Don't make it longer than three sentences. Do the same with the three petitions of the penitential rite. After you have written the first version, go over it and begin to take words out and to change other words from Latin roots to Anglo-Saxon. Do this twice. You will be amazed at how you begin to look at words to see what is their power to deliver fast and hard. Do the same thing with your sermon. You will be delighted with the result. The people will be overwhelmed with joy!

Winston Churchill's memorable statement says it all: "Give me the arms and I will do the job." This is a classic example of a careful use of the words that communicate best. He did not say some or other version of the following: "Deliver to my disposal the suitable and sufficient implements of warfare and I shall expedite the venture with a view to complete success."

Christiane Brusselmans, internationally acclaimed catechist, says over and over that the language of teaching should be simple, concrete and poetic. *Simple* would mean short, direct words rather than many-syllable words. Simple would mean short, declarative sentences as opposed to long sentences with lots of phrases and clauses. Too many of us tend to preach in the style in which we used to write essays. The habit is hard to break. We should know by now that lots of clauses and participles are excellent Latin style. Cicero would rejoice. But these constructions are poor style for communicating the American style of spoken and written English. When we say it simply, in short words and quick sentences, we say it strong and loud and clear.

Our preaching should be *concrete*. That means using lots of clear images whenever we can. We need to express concepts and ideas, but they need not be put forth in conceptual language all the time.

For a long time I used conceptual language in wonderfully assembled logical sequence. Then I found out that I was just being too lazy to look for the concrete, strong images that say it so much better. I began to change my style, and it has paid off. I preach well now, better than ever before, and the switch to simple language and concrete images has a lot to do with it. A good case in point is how we might talk about Jesus, the God-man. We can talk about him in the language of Aristotelian philosophy, in terms of nature and substance and essence and hylomorphism. We can talk about divine nature and human nature finding unity and being subsumed into one person. We can talk about matter and about form and such, or we can use the more complex language of recent European theologians and philosophers. But none of this gives people even a glimpse of who Jesus is and what he is all about.

We can help people get to know Jesus by speaking about Jesus in the language of the Bible, by preaching about the different names and titles of Jesus in both Old and New Testaments. Jesus is son . . . he is brother . . . bread and wine . . . and the way . . . the life and light . . . Messiah . . . the new Moses . . . we could go on and on. Christiane Brusselmans is forever pointing out that preaching the names of Jesus leads to all kinds of good results. When we preach the names of Jesus, we must use concrete images instead of ideas. We open up the many dimensions of Jesus.

This tends to bring him from "out there" to "in here," right close beside me. Preaching the names of Jesus helps people to identify with Jesus much faster and much more closely. These names of Jesus are what people hear in the gospel. They become familiar with the names and are delighted with this familiarity. Finally, preaching the names of Jesus leads to all kinds of creative expression. We can sing his names, dance them, make poetry of them. How delightful a song is "Lord of the Dance"! How much sound theology it expresses! Can you imagine singing about substance and nature and hypostatic union?

When we make our preaching simple and concrete and full of images, we are already making it *poetic.* When we use the word "poetic" here, we are not attempting to infringe on the art of poetry itself. We are thinking in the much wider context of simple language and strong image. Shakespeare does it well.

It helps no end to have a sense of humor!

We can't get that close, and some of his work would not be our best model. But we can keep trying. It is amazing what can break through when we keep working at it. Please try.

When you preach, tell the story. Tell it the way you tell a story. You have many stories to tell: Jesus' story, the church's story, your story. Often these stories are all mixed into one; that is just fine as long as you have the feel of telling the story. That's how you give Jesus and yourself to your people all together at once. Jesus' story is your story; your story is Jesus' story and the story of all the people with whom you are talking. Remember: your personal and human presence is essential. Through personal presence you identify with your people, and you invite them to identify with you. If there is no identification, there is little or no communication. People simply do not know how to identify with an "infallible" figure. They just admire, which means they stay at a distance. Distance is far, far away from presence.

In preaching at Sunday Mass, you do everyone a great service by limiting your preaching to the space of ten minutes. Work hard at this. If people can count on the preaching to be of humanly tolerable duration, they will begin to trust you and be ready to listen. Reasonable length in the homily will permit all the other important elements of the celebration to be at their best.

When we preach and preside well, we get what a good life-giving celebration is all about: a balanced experience of a gathered community sharing. It has structure and shape, and all assembly members have a chance to speak their parts. A well-prepared Sunday celebration with good balance among its parts is an exciting experience. For too long we made Sunday Mass the occasion or backdrop for a sermon. Now we know better. We know we must balance the entire celebration very carefully. We know we are prone to verbal overkill, so we are careful about that. We give people time to breathe and really be part of the celebration.

This ideal of balance requires, of course, that the other signs of the celebration really are life-giving. It takes the energy of a lot of people, working as a team, to make a life-giving celebration. But, as we said in the very beginning, word and sacrament are equally important parts of Sunday Mass. They go hand in hand; they depend on one another. When one fails, the other is diminished. That is why I got around to writing this book on preaching and teaching after I had written considerably about the theology and practice of sacramental celebration. It was inevitable.

CONCLUSION

Yes, this really is the end! We learn to give homilies by giving them often and by working on them seriously. In the preparing and giving of homilies, we are not afraid of making mistakes. We are willing to go to the scripture texts themselves day after day to see what we can make of them. We use the helps that are available without becoming slaves to homily aids. We avoid canned stuff like the plague. Nothing substitutes for our own personal, daily meditative learning and reading and speaking and living the word of the Lord.

The homilist starts with the word of God, rejoices in it, savors it, praises it, celebrates it and proclaims it, then goes on to open up an insight that is present in the word. The homilist then tries to discover and open up what meaning that insight has for those particular people at this specific point in time. The homily, as a carefully orchestrated part of the celebration, leads the people to a more fruitful experience in this Mass and to a life of greater service to brothers and sisters outside. The homily is speaking and hearing a word, with all that this means.

I would like to sum it up this way. God for us is life giver and lover. God sent Jesus to be life giver and lover. Jesus did a good job of it. Jesus now sends his church to be life giver and lover. That means us. We who are called to give life to brothers and sisters must make life-giving and loving signs. When we make life-giving signs, we have to put ourselves into them. We have to give of ourselves. That is what being a Christian is all about. And it helps no end to have a sense of humor!

We who are called to give life to brothers and sisters must make life-giving and loving signs. When we make life-giving signs, we have to put ourselves into them. We have to give of ourselves.

Page 173 top Eugene Aloysius Walsh *(right)* and friend at Saint Charles College, Catonsville, Maryland, 1930

Page 173 bottom Gene during seminary studies (1931 – 1938) at The Catholic University of America, Washington, DC, residing at the Sulpician Theological College

Page 174 top Gene's ordination to the presbyterate, Baltimore, Maryland, June 7, 1938

Page 174 bottom In 1940s, with students at Saint Mary's Seminary on Paca Street, Baltimore, where for 26 years Gene directed music and taught courses in philosophy, education, sacraments and faith

Page 175 top With students at Paca Street

Page 175 bottom During 1950s, Gene and choir providing music for television programs

Page 176 top With his mother Mary Agnes "Mamie" Walsh a year before her 1966 death

Page 176 bottom Last time Gene presided for Mass, 1989

Page 177 top (left to right) John Broadbent (seminary director, Dunedin, New Zealand), Fred J. Nijem (pastor of Sacred Heart Church, Warner Robins, Georgia), Leonard Anthony Boyle (bishop of Dunedin, New Zealand) and Gene

Page 177 bottom On the way to Rotorura, New Zealand: Gene, Peter McCormick (seminary director, Palmerston North, New Zealand) and Ruth Eger (friend)

Page 178 top Ann Burke (friend), Gene, Elaine Rendler (liturgical musician), John Buscemi (liturgical artist) and James Burke (friend)

Page 178 bottom Gene

*If we are willing
and able to pass on
our soundly based
speculation to the
next generation, we
are going to save
them from a lot of the
foolishness we had
to work through as
we struggled toward
an adult faith.*

PART 3

Talking about Eugene Walsh

1
WHAT I LEARNED FROM GENE WALSH

Tom Conry

It is strange and instructive that, in America, iconic figures are routinely reinterpreted as less threatening (and less interesting) after their deaths.

Consider the example of Dr. Martin Luther King, Jr., who spent years opposing not only racism but also militarism and unrestrained capitalism. He was repeatedly (and illegally) wiretapped by the FBI on the authority of that notorious autocrat, J. Edgar Hoover. Dr. King made speech after speech opposing the war in Vietnam, claiming that racism could never be eradicated until capitalism and militarism were rooted out. All this is a matter of record.

But in the popular imagination all that has been conveniently forgotten now, and Dr. King's message has been watered down in favor of a benign and familiar sentimentality. At the civic celebrations surrounding the holiday marking his birth, it is now hard to distinguish Dr. King's radically prophetic convictions from the banal pronouncements of, say, Rodney King: "Can't we all just get along?"

That process of myth-making is exceptional because in the rest of the world, it seems to go the other way. Iconic figures become more radical — not more centrist — after their martyrdoms.

Salvador Allende of Chile, Oscar Romero of El Salvador, and more recently Luis Renaldo Colosio of Mexico are all examples of moderate leftists who became profoundly more radical in the popular imagination after their deaths.

Here in the United States it is just the opposite. Here, figures like Dorothy Day and Helen Keller are routinely domesticated and rendered palatable for purposes of marketing. Their fundamental political character is discarded. They are reinterpreted as moralizing agents. They become comfortable grist for our pandemic civil religion that celebrates them as plucky sentimentalists rather than dangerous organizers for social change.

> *Perhaps the contribution for which Gene is best known is his insistence on ritual hospitality. He maintained that nothing in the Mass could be divine if it was not first of all authentically human.*

This process of myth-making is instructive because it tells us everything about what it comforts us to believe, what we in fact *need* to believe, about our heroes and about ourselves. We love the paradigm of the hero because it reassures us that someone can do something to affect those institutions that extend their subtle but implacable control over our lives. We love the myth of the hero because we can participate vicariously, without excessive personal risk or commitment. Most of all, we love the myth of the hero because we can control the myth in a way we could never control the person.

For many of us who have been leading music in parishes, Gene Walsh was that kind of iconic figure. He spent most of his life teaching in seminaries, yet clearly identified himself with unordained musicians. He spoke out consistently on behalf of music and musicians, even when it was unfashionable to do so. At a time in which the liturgical rhetoric was dominated by those who wished to scold the assembly for not accepting this or that liturgical change, Gene spoke clearly and directly about the obligation that liturgical ministers had to put some life into their liturgical celebrations.

In short, he was a lifelong teacher of presiders who allied himself with the cause of the assembly.

Now we are in the process of reinterpreting Gene's work. Perhaps inevitably, in the process of trying to make it accessible, we are taking away his hard edges, remaking him into a kindly old gentleman who merely asked that we pay more attention to one another in Mass. His insistence on the radical equality between presider and assembly, his proposal to restructure the opening rite by eliminating the procession, his tenacity in seeking a real partnership between musicians and presiders, all are gradually receding in the popular imagination. Gene is becoming just another nice guy. Let me give you an example of how this happens.

I can remember sitting with Gene in the lounge at the Portland State University Campus Ministry Center in the summer of 1988. I asked him what he was lecturing on nowadays. He said that he was speaking out against the "spirituality" movement (as in: "a spirituality for lectors" or "a spirituality for eucharistic ministers"). He said that no such thing existed and that it was simply (I am trying to remember his exact words now) a cynical attempt to sell something other than the gospel which is freely and universally available to everyone.

In *Proclaiming God's Love in Word and Deed,* Gene says:

> **There is no spirituality specifically for readers,**
> **gospel proclaimers, pastoral musicians or anyone**
> **else in the assembly. Why? Because there is one**
> **Christ, one Holy Spirit and one faith.**[1]

This is central to what my experience was of Gene's way of thinking about the liturgy. He believed that the entire concept of "spirituality" was flawed. You can see some of this in how he wrote about the basic "sound" that was necessary and appropriate to lead the assembly in song:

> Our music traditions of the recent past come out of too great an emphasis on the sacred over the profane. We have suffered as a result . . . I think the boy soprano sound is fine and I support the successful efforts of many to develop it. But I find no reason to claim it as a more valid church sound than mixed or female voices. It is all part of the vague but strong prejudice that accepts the disembodied sound as more "spiritual." Personally I think it is part of the Platonic idea that the height of religious piety is reached when the spirit triumphs over flesh and we all become angels.[2]

In the face of this process of reinterpretation, I want to write down a few of the things that I learned from Gene and tell a few of the stories of how I came to learn them.

Gene Walsh was so ubiquitous in the early days of the liturgical reform movement that everybody has stories like these. I can't claim a unique personal relationship with him. But he was my friend and teacher, impatient with mediocrity, angry with stupidity and venality, and he spent his life fighting against those who said we couldn't do any better than this.

LESSON ONE: LET THE ASSEMBLY BE THE ASSEMBLY

Gene really believed all that stuff about baptism to which so many of us pay mere lip service. He genuinely believed that the assembly was the primary minister of the eucharist. He held that this principle had actual ritual consequences.

For example, Gene adamantly opposed vesting unordained ministers. He correctly understood that, whatever their protestations to the contrary, those who wish to dress up cantors, choirs, eucharistic ministers, lectors, etc. in albs or other robe-like garments are actually trying to re-establish ordination as the necessary pre-condition of liturgical ministry. He used to refer to this practice as "playing dress-up."

To understand the impulse behind this practice, you have to understand the "sponge theory" of liturgical power.

The "sponge theory" argues that all the ritual power that matters rests, as a matter of fact, with the presider. Instead of addressing this problem directly, "sponge theory" enthusiasts seek to finesse it by (for example) lining up the lectors and eucharistic ministers and placing them in the entrance procession (there it is again!), dressing them up in quasi-ritual clothing derived from the presider's vestments, etc. In a well-intentioned effort to indicate that these ministries are important they perhaps even give them some distinctive medallion, or find ways to seat them up in the altar area with the presider — all of this in the hope that some of the liturgical power will "drip off" of the ordained one and be "sponged up" by the other ministers.

Gene resolutely opposed the "sponge theory" of empowering the different liturgical ministries. For example, he claimed, "First, readers are seated in the assembly. This is the proper place . . . The ministry of reading God's word is not a clerical ministry but belongs to the people."[3] He insisted that all ministries — including the ones associated with ordination — evolve out of baptism, and that this had to be shown in an unmistakable way in the Sunday liturgy.

All parishes are faced with a set of ritual problems to solve, involving the issue of who is integral to the ritual and who is extraneous. These problems flow from the very architecture of our ritual space with its artificial division between the sanctuary area (for the ordained) and the nave area (for the non-ordained). They stem from an inadequate ecclesiology which claimed for years that only an ordained person was necessary to celebrate the Mass.

These problems and their inadequate solutions are displayed each week in the opening rite, sometimes tellingly referred to as the entrance rite. The people have presumably already "entered" their space, so whose entrance are we talking about, anyway?

As Gene pointed out on numerous occasions, in many parishes the Mass begins when the presider simply appears in the back of the church building, often without any prior relationship with the assembly. Typically, he is preceded by the ritually important symbol of the cross and a couple of servers dressed in vestments suggestive of a "junior clergy" status. The assembly observes this procession, which is clearly the remnant of an earlier Carolingian royalism. The length of the singing is most often determined by how long it takes the presider to take his rightful place near the ritually important furniture.

What's wrong with this picture?

Minutes into this kind of liturgy it has become clear that our practical ideology is that baptism is inferior to ordination. Ordination is where the power is. The assembly has been rendered a client class, a colony — consumers of an event manufactured by others.

Gene vigorously opposed all this. I think he spoke more about the opening rite than about anything else, and the common element in all of his speaking and writings was that, until the assembly's baptism is experienced in a practical way as the equal of the presider's ordination, the promise of the reformed liturgy will never be fulfilled.

LESSON TWO: GOOD RITUAL IS NOT NECESSARILY WHAT'S IN THE BOOK

Which is to say, ritual ought to be judged on its results. That which is life-giving is ritually useful. That which is death-dealing ought to be discarded.

186

This is a terrifying thought for a lot of liturgical types. I have actually heard an acquaintance of mine — a man with a doctorate in liturgy, who ought to know better — exclaim in a fit of exasperation, "Why can't they just take what's in the book and do it well?" Gene would always insist, "Good liturgy is not in the book."

The best and funniest example of these two contrasting attitudes about what makes up good liturgy came when Gene, Elaine Rendler, Jim Hansen and I were in New Orleans for an NPM regional convention in the sweltering July of 1986. We had left the elegant conference hotel to take a walk and wound up in a pretty tough part of town. We stopped in our tracks when we encountered a group of teenage street musicians playing an unaffected, powerful jazz that had clearly not been refined for the tourist trade. I remember Gene saying that if God were anywhere in the neighborhood he was here with these kids rather than back at the elegant Clarion hotel.

So we took up a collection among the four of us and came up with eighty bucks, slipped it to the trumpet player, and asked them to show up at the panel discussion we were supposed to have that night. We guessed they'd probably pocket the money and not show up, but we figured we were contributing to a good cause in any event.

So there were Elaine, Jim, Gene and I making The Usual Pronouncements about The Usual Stuff, when one of the suits from the hotel walked in and demanded to know who was in charge. He looked very nervous. Apparently a bunch of musicians had gathered just outside in the hotel lobby that — how can I put this delicately? — didn't look like they belonged.

It was just about then that the band entered playing a version of "When the Saints Go Marchin' In" that lifted all people in that conference room out of their seats.

I mean, the space itself simply erupted. People were dancing on the tables. A glass pitcher was passed overhead for the musicians in the middle of all this bedlam; people were stuffing in their tens and twenties until the pitcher couldn't hold any more. Another was found. More music, more bedlam.

In the center of this chaos, Gene was smiling with a beatific radiance. He walked over and shouted in my ear, "This is the real liturgy for this convention."

That was as happy as I ever saw Gene Walsh. Life had broken through. Gene was always on the side of life, whether it came out of the book or not. He believed that there had to be spaces for people to express how they really felt in any kind of ritual, and that an important part of how one evaluated whether ritual was life-giving or death-dealing lay in whether this was allowed to happen.

LESSON THREE: RITUAL IS INHERENTLY INTERESTING

What mattered to Gene was life. I heard Gene say many times that the defining characteristic of the great majority of parish liturgies was boredom. And, as far as I was able to tell, what bothered Gene more than anything else in the world was that we simply accepted this as inevitable.

As to the origins of this boredom, there are two theories.

Theory A holds that the liturgy is an inherently uninteresting experience. Those who believe this seek to find interesting albeit non-ritual elements to rescue us from our collective lack of interest. Accordingly, they're big on processions (which Gene generally opposed), strong on carrying the book at the exact angle calculated to invoke awe and respect. They believe that there is hardly a liturgical problem that can't be solved with better vestments, a generous dollop of incense and louder hymnody. They take as authority not a genuine tradition but rather a big red book and an attendant collection of statements commissioned by bishops and written to episcopal specifications. They are looking for the loopholes where they can stick something, anything, that will relieve the tedium.

Theory B holds that, while ritual prayer may be at any given moment (in Ralph Keifer's phrase) "inherently monotonous," that is not the same as being simply boring. The adherents of Theory B believe that ritual gathers meaning through repetition. Theory B respects the ability of the assembly to integrate complex imagery and interpret that imagery in terms of its own experience over time. Those who believe this have confidence that the assembly is capable of listening attentively to the proclamation of the word if the word is simply read in a clear and straightforward way. They believe that the stories of sharing and redemption which make up the service of the table are intelligible and available to the assembly if they are merely presented fairly.

Gene was an advocate of Theory B; he believed that "originality" is the enemy of ritual, and represented an insufficient trust that the ritual itself had the power to hold the assembly's attention. He believed that much of the conservative opposition to the liturgical reform was in fact resentment of this "originality" . . . he used to regularly chuckle at the latest stories of the balloons and butterflies crowd. He spoke against the use of "theme" for Sunday liturgies. He knew that this represented more than anything a failure of nerve. In the words of critic John Willett:

"For as soon as anyone is moved by a communicative impulse that is stronger than himself, then he can forget about 'originality'; that pathetic ideal of the arts in our time. He uses a vocabulary which people will understand, and however highly educated he is he needs all his wits and all his artistry to convey his point."[4]

Gene advocated using "the fewest words, and with as many words of Anglo-Saxon origin as possible. Anglo-Saxon words communicate much more powerfully than do words of Latin origin."[5] He believed that liturgical preparation generally meant taking things out of the liturgy, not putting more things in. For example, he proposed dropping the Gloria, reducing the size of the penitential rite and singing a closing hymn only on special occasions. He believed that no one came to Mass in order to avoid encountering Jesus. He believed that if the ritual clutter were cleared away, people would embrace the questions proposed by the word and the table. He believed in the people.

LESSON FOUR: QUESTION AUTHORITY, ESPECIALLY YOUR OWN

I remember very well a surprising conversation that I had with Gene at the 1981 NPM national convention in Detroit. Gene was holding forth in the hospitality suite about any number of things and a group of folks was gathered around to hear what he had to say.

At one point a young woman asked him what he thought about the gospel acclamation, gospel processions and such.

In short, he was a lifelong teacher of presiders who allied himself with the cause of the assembly.

Gene declared that they ought to be dropped altogether, that they conveyed the impression that the other readings were somehow a mere preface to the Gospel, and that they were the product of a subtle anti-Semitism. A lively discussion followed, and Gene refused to back down.

After the group had broken up, I pointed out that this was the exact opposite of what he had said at a conference some years earlier in Baltimore. Gene looked at me with absolute sincerity and said, "Well, yes, that's what I *used* to believe *then!*"

I guess at this point Gene was about seventy years old. He had simply never accepted that the answers that he had given at one time were the answers forever. He believed that the liturgical renewal was still in its infancy, that it had to grow, change, listen to its own experience. As far as I can tell, he never fell victim to his own dogma, but remained open to new insights throughout his entire life.

LESSON FIVE: HOSPITALITY IS THE PRECONDITION OF RITUAL

Perhaps the contribution for which Gene is best known is his insistence on ritual hospitality. He maintained that nothing in the Mass could be divine if it was not first of all authentically human. He often used to cite the story in Luke of the woman in the house of Simon the Pharisee as an example of what Jesus himself thought was crucial at the eucharistic meal.

Then [Jesus] gestured toward the woman and said to Simon, "Do you see her? When I came into your house, you did not give me water to wash my feet, but she has bathed them with her own tears and wiped them with her own hair. You did not kiss me, but she has not stopped kissing my feet since I came in. You did not anoint my head with oil, but she anointed my feet with ointment." (Luke 7:44–46)

In my opinion, this idea of ritual hospitality has been largely misunderstood as merely being nice to one another before the Mass begins. In fact, it is a subtly different and subversively powerful strategy for being church in what Christopher Lasch called "the culture of narcissism."

What Gene advocated by liturgical hospitality was nothing less than changing how people expected to act when they went to church. He simply proposed that we begin to acknowledge one another, not as individuals whom we may like or dislike, but as members of the assembly, the tribe, the people.

It is the lack of the assembly's experience of itself as an assembly that Gene thought was at the root of most of our liturgical difficulties. If we could somehow break through the assembly's American privatism and disarm its expectation of a cloistered religious experience, then the Sunday Mass could return to its traditional task of serving communities rather than individuals.

As Mark Searle has written:

> Full participation was one of the battle cries of the liturgical movement and one of the guiding principles of the liturgical reform. It is rooted in the fact that God does not choose and save individuals as such, but that he has created and is creating a people for himself, to witness as a community in the midst of a divided and antagonistic world. It was because the old Latin liturgy did not adequately express that, although it was full of vestiges of such awareness, that it had to be revised. The revision of texts and the promulgation of new rubrics was a comparatively simple matter. It is quite a different matter — and a far more difficult one, we are discovering — to develop the corresponding attitudes and acquire a sense of ourselves as a people.
>
> Until that does happen, however, the liturgy will never quite come alive. Until active participation in the liturgy becomes simply one manifestation of active participation in the common life of the People of God, it will be done by rote and without conviction.[6]

It was for this very practical reason that Gene advocated engaging people in conversation prior to the Mass both inside and outside of the church building. He knew that since the basic requirement for the ritual is that the people would be effectively gathered — that is, that they would recognize themselves as a community, not as a collection of individuals — then those who hoped that the liturgy would succeed needed to change the expected behavior of Massgoers. They might arrive as individuals, but somehow or another they must be transformed into a people if the Lord's Supper is to be celebrated effectively.

LESSON LAST: IT GOES BY QUICK. MAKE IT COUNT.

A few days after what turned out to be his seventy-eighth and last birthday, Gene and I went to dinner in Baltimore. Gene was talking about his experiences in the early days of the postconciliar reform movement. He talked about what he had hoped for out of the liturgical reform, and how disappointed he was in the manner in which many parishes had responded to those reforms.

I asked him how long it felt, subjectively, since he was my age (at that time, thirty-seven years old). He considered the question for some time and finally, looking me straight in the eye, simply snapped his fingers.

That was the last time I saw Gene.

The day Gene died, I was teaching Scripture at an NPM Cantor School at Pacific Lutheran University in Tacoma, Washington. The group decided to have a memorial service. We climbed a long, winding staircase to the University's chapel and we read the passage from 2 Kings 2 in which Elijah is taken up to heaven in a whirlwind of fire before his student and heir, the prophet Elisha.

In the five years that have followed, I have reflected on the ironic suitability of that reading more than once. You see, Elijah and Elisha were the last authentic members of the independent guild prophets of Israel.

Guild prophets first appeared at the time of Saul's accession to the leadership of Israel in about 1020 BCE. These guild prophets were called the "Sons of Prophets" *(Bene haNebi'im),* an idiomatic Hebrew expression designating those associated with a prophet or those enrolled in a prophetic "school."

These roving bands of prophets trafficked in ecstasy. It was said that they sang and danced so powerfully that no one could resist them. And the greatest of all the masters of the guild prophets were Elijah and Elisha, who apparently engineered the bloody end of King Ahab and his consort Jezebel. They saw themselves not only as musicians but as the embodiment of political resistance against an oppressive monarchical caste.

Soon after the time of Elijah and Elisha, there was a break in the guild prophet tradition. The guild prophets became "state" prophets beholden to the king. Their function seems to have been to "prophesy" on demand for whoever was writing their paycheck. They wrote and sang the king's songs; they danced for the greater honor and glory of the royal establishment. They finally became a wholly owned subsidiary of the monarchy.

I guess that's how I think about us as liturgical musicians these days. Now we who were once the principal prophetic presence acting on behalf of the liturgical reform, whose music once set the popular agenda for that reform — we ourselves have become the surrogates of the enemies of the liturgical reform by refusing to challenge them directly. Like the guild prophets of old we have become more and more mere henchmen of the people who sign our paychecks, singing their songs, uncritically legitimizing their message, accepting their agenda.

Anyone who doubts that this is the case ought to simply page through the music that is ordinarily sung in our parishes and ask: Where are the songs that women can sing about what is happening to them in the church these days? Where is the music that calls us out of our romantic infatuation with religion and enables us to acknowledge how tough it is to get up and go to Mass in the present ecclesial situation? Hardly a week goes by without some new assault on the revolution of Vatican II, not only in the liturgical arena but in others as well. Where are the songs that engage this?

Some of these songs exist. In a few places some of them are even sung. But by and large the music that will turn the tide in these struggles is yet to be written. At the end of his life, Gene was longing to sing those songs.

Gene admired musicians and liked to be around them. But more than that, Gene knew that in most parishes the liturgical musicians, instrumentalists and singers, were the engine of liturgical reform. It was the musicians who disproportionately organized and served on the liturgical committees, trained the lectors, baked the bread and generally made the wheels turn. They were the infantry of the postconciliar reform and even now, tellingly enough, perhaps four out of five people who make their living as parish liturgists are also musicians.

As for me, I am still looking toward the day when Gene's vision of a church of hospitality, truthfulness and honor can come to be. But frankly, it's harder without him. With all my heart I believe that Gene is risen, alive, but we could sure use him in the flesh these days. He would have something to say now as he did then about our abject capitulation in the face of ecclesial difficulties.

In the meantime, I am just like you.

> Every day, to earn my daily bread
> I go to the market where lies are bought.
> Hopefully
> I take up my place among the sellers.[7]
>
> — Bertolt Brecht

---

1 Eugene Walsh, *Proclaiming God's Love in Word and Deed* (Portland OR: OCP Publications, 1994) 84.

2 Eugene Walsh, *Proclaiming God's Love in Song* (Portland OR: OCP Publications, 1994) 52–53.

3 *Proclaiming God's Love in Word and Deed,* 70.

4 John Willett, *The Theater of Bertolt Brecht* (New York: New Directions, 1959) 225.

5 Gene Walsh, *Proclaiming God's Love in Song* (Portland OR: OCP Publications, 1994) 28.

6 Mark Searle, *Liturgy Made Simple* (Collegeville: The Liturgical Press, 1981) 90.

7 Bertolt Brecht, "Hollywood," in *Poems 1913–1956*, John Willett and Ralph Manheim, editors, with the cooperation of Erich Fried (New York: Methuen, 1976) 382.

Tom Conry, music minister for the Newman Center at the University of Minnesota, is an acclaimed composer, workshop presenter, defender of the poor and promoter of justice. He has published numerous collections of liturgical music with OCP Publications.

2

"YOU ARE AS GOOD A LOVER AS YOU ARE A SIGN MAKER."

Virgil C. Funk

The time was 11:15 A.M. It was November, 1957, and Father Gene Walsh was teaching a course on the history of education to 43 third-year college seminarians called, in those days, first-year philosophers. All seminarians were dressed in cassocks, as was "Geno" (the nickname given him by the students), only our cassocks were still new, while the material in Geno's cassock was shiny from wear.

He was outlining on the blackboard the goals of education in different Western societies and showing how the central aim of Spartan education included warlike discipline, while Athenian education modified its chief goal to include athletic discipline. Geno turned to the class of seminarians and asked them pointedly, "And what do you believe to be the goal of your education — just rote memory of philosophical truths, or learning how to think for yourselves?" This was rich fare for the fertile minds of nineteen-year-olds, many of whom had been trained at a minor seminary specializing in the memorization of Greek and Latin vocabulary. Then his thoughts began to pour out of him: "If you are to become an adult, you must let go of your childhood. You must take risks. The rites of the church's liturgy are not to enslave you, but to lead you to freedom. What type of faith do you have? Aren't you aware of the renewal of the liturgy that is taking place which will provide a freeing experience in your prayer life?" As the ideas and questions flowed and connected to one another, it became clear to me that Geno was combining the Greek notion of excellence (*arete*[1]) in education with an ideal of the human person, with contemporary issues, with the liturgical renewal . . . and with what was my developing ideal of what it took to be fully human. Three or four ideas overlaid each other in his exhortation, and his questions were bound to produce an insight in anyone open to the challenge of his teaching.

> *The roots of all that Gene was to do in liturgy and spirituality in the United States are to be found in his ability to teach.*

And in the midst of connecting *arete* with personal goals and the renewal of the liturgy, Geno would insert his own thinking about Bernard Lonergan's recent book *Insight*. Lonergan's long and complicated theory of human understanding, which mixed mathematical formulas and philosophical sophistication, was beyond the minds of most of the people in Geno's class, but we could see (literally) what insight was, because Gene was having one — or several — as he taught. He was exploding with creativity while he was teaching.

———————

I was delighted to be asked to reflect with you, the reader of these challenging writings of Father Gene Walsh, about his place in the liturgical-spiritual movement in the United States. I was a student in his two courses on the history and philosophy of education in 1957–58 and 1958–59; I was one of the four members of his schola, a member of his seminary choir and secretary-librarian for his choir during those same years at St. Mary's Seminary on Paca Street in Baltimore, Maryland. I had Gene as my confessor and spiritual director as well, and remained one of his lifelong companions in the work of liturgical renewal until his death in 1989.

———————

BEFORE THE COUNCIL

A bit of the history of the liturgical movement might be helpful in understanding what Gene Walsh accomplished.[2] The period from 1909 to 1963 was a period of intense ferment for those interested in renewing the church's worship. It began with Lambert Beauduin's call for a liturgical movement and ended with the opening session of the Second Vatican Council. This was also a time of great tension in the church, especially in the seminary environment, between those in favor of the liturgical movement (a very small number) and those who wanted things to stay the way they were (a very large number).

In the United States, building on the groundwork of Dom Virgil Michel, who had died in 1938, the liturgical movement crystallized in the National Liturgical Weeks (soon sponsored by The Liturgical Conference[3]) which began in 1940 and were held every year thereafter until 1969. In 1949, Gene obtained his doctorate in philosophy; his dissertation examined the sacramental theology of French spiritual writers of the late 1890s.[4] His research had brought him into contact with the German theologians Karl Adam and Dom Odo Casel, both of whom influenced Walsh's thinking and writing,[5] and Romano Guardini's essay "Man is God's Way to Man," which was foundational for Gene's emerging understanding of humanity.

In 1953 Gene Walsh attended his first National Liturgical Week and was elected to the board of directors of The Liturgical Conference the next year. He was an important figure at those meetings into the late 1960s. He gave presentations at the 1957 and 1958 Weeks and was deeply involved in the planning of the music used at those gatherings. Omer Westendorf prepared for presentation at the 1958 Week the first version of *Our Parish Prays and Sings* (Collegeville: The Liturgical Press, 1959), the first English-language hymnal designed for contemporary liturgical

199

celebrations, for which Gene was one of the major consultors and an ardent promoter following the 1958 Week. While most of the board of The Liturgical Conference were priests of German descent who were working as pastors, Gene, who was of Irish descent, represented the link between seminary and parish, between theory and practice, between the German mystics and the Irish pragmatists. Faculty from seminaries were rarely seen at such progressive meetings.

During this pre-Vatican II period, Gene did not teach liturgy in the classroom; most liturgy classes in those days amounted to a study of the rubrics. But he was the director of the seminary choir and through that medium introduced the choir members to the rationale behind a new and untested repertoire of contemporary music for worship — some with English texts — while exposing the student body and reluctant faculty members to changes which seem minuscule to post-Vatican II hindsight but which at the time seemed like an overthrow of the entire "ordinary way of doing business." We sang the psalms of Joseph Gelineau and works of other contemporary European composers such as Jean Langlais, Flor Peeters and Jan Nieland, and joined in standard "Catholic" hymns — "Praise to the Lord" and "To Jesus Christ Our Sovereign King" — which we sang at "low" Mass. These were revolutionary in an all-Latin environment. Chant was still dominant, but few seminarians who were at St. Mary's, Paca Street, in that era will forget the thrill of processing, vested in cassock, surplice and biretta, into the reverberating seminary chapel as we sang the haunting strains of the Gelineau antiphon for Psalm 122: "We shall go up with joy to the house of our God." No matter how beautiful the Gregorian setting of the Latin antiphon for Psalm 122, *Laetatus sum*, might sound, it did not have the impact that this type of music did when used to assist the ritual procession into chapel. Gene believed in learning by doing.

Gene was dedicated to introducing a sung liturgy and developed and promoted the use of four vernacular hymns at the entrance, offertory, communion and recessional.[6] His understanding was that the chants used at these points in the Latin liturgy served to accompany the four processions of the Mass — the entrance of the ministers, the presentation of gifts, the procession of the assembly to communion and the exit of the ministers — and that each hymn should function as an expression of the appropriate procession. Usually, at his direction, this ritual function was respected. But in the hands of amateurs beyond the seminary, singing *at* these four moments of the liturgy came to dominate the singing *of* the liturgy, and the four-hymn Mass became a symbol for misunderstanding the ritual function of music in the liturgy. Gene often admitted the mistake this innovation turned out to be!

In the time before the council, Gene was one of about 500 people in the United States who were totally committed to liturgical renewal and, eventually, to a total reform of the liturgy's structures and texts. He held to this position in spite of strong opposition from fellow priests on the faculty, sometimes enduring rejection and ridicule by them, and he remained not only an advocate but also an experimenter, especially in music, with new forms of liturgical celebrations. His friends Joe Connolly and Joe Gallagher were diocesan priests of Baltimore working outside the seminary. Both were highly political men. Connolly became the president of The Liturgical Conference in the late 1960s, with Gene always serving as his advisor; Gallagher was the editor of the archdiocesan paper, *The Catholic Review*, who resigned his editorship over a disagreement with his archbishop concerning the freedom of the press and declined the title of monsignor because of his disagreement with *Humanae Vitae*. Gene never sought to be a public dissident or president of anything, but he was always present to and supportive of his friends as they took such positions.

Gene's biographer, Timothy Leonard, ends his biography by emphasizing Gene's ability to teach:

> **The lives of teachers need to be told because they are an integral part of cultural history. Teachers do not lead people into battle, they do not sign treaties or make laws; nor do they necessarily lead lives of great scholarship. But they catch the sense of what is moving forward, grasp the meaning of their times and mediate that meaning to their students. Such a teacher was Eugene Walsh, and a very good one at that.**[7]

The roots of all that Gene was to do in liturgy and spirituality in the United States are to be found in his ability to teach.

VATICAN II

The second phase of the liturgical movement began with the Second Vatican Council's endorsement of the Constitution on the Sacred Liturgy in 1963 and the subsequent implementation of vernacular translations of the revised *Roman Lectionary for Mass* and the *Sacramentary* completed in 1969.

This was a period when preconciliar outcasts became the favorite children of the church. Gene Walsh moved from a marginal position as a teacher of the philosophy of education to a central post as the rector of Theological College, the national seminary associated with The Catholic University of America in Washington, D.C. It was during his time at "T.C." that Gene first began to teach liturgy in a formal way, concentrating especially on the liturgy practicum (how to preside at Mass) for the seminarians.

Gene's ability to maintain a confrontative edge, never far out of sight, now grew sharper, reinforced with the vindicating authority of the Council. Unfortunately, Gene's administrative ability didn't develop as sharply. The turbulence of the Kennedy and King assassinations, the civil rights riots in Washington within view of the back window of the seminary, gave impetus to ever more radical reform by the seminarians and their rector, but the reformers did not hold a mutually agreed-upon vision. So while the second phase of the liturgical movement was a time of great success in implementing the renewal for most of those interested in liturgical renewal, this was a period of turbulence and disappointment for Gene. Eventually, he resigned as rector of the seminary, unable to accomplish the implementation of the vision of which he had long dreamed, at least within the seminary system. Quite frankly, there were too many explosions going off at any one time for him to control, and he retired from seminary work in 1974.

IMPLEMENTING THE RENEWAL

The third phase of the liturgical movement began in 1970 and continued through 1990: a period of implementing the renewal in the parish. I remember clearly Gene's answer to a question placed to him in 1959 by a fellow seminarian who asked him, "What would you *really* like to do?" Without batting an eye, Gene responded, "I want one of you to become a bishop and invite me into your diocese, where I can try to implement these ideas in practice."

Gene didn't exactly respond to an episcopal mandate after his retirement as rector of Theological College, but he did hook up with a parish in Northern Virginia (St. Mark's in Vienna), where he began to modify the material he had been presenting to seminarians for the previous thirty years into language (non-Latin-based words, "good Anglo-Saxon words," he would say) that was immediately understandable to the typical parishioner. He met with his good friend and former student Dan Onley, and Dan began publishing his ideas in brief inexpensive pamphlets. Almost instantly, a new career began for Gene. With over 1,000 of his former students serving as ordained priests, Gene moved across the United States giving parish retreats, liturgical days and weekend study programs to parishes of every size and shape. He was willing to work anywhere, but he loved the water, so the mainland East Coast and West Coast, and especially the islands of Hawaii, were favorite spots he revisited often.

The central ideas that had guided his life were transformed into a working popular language: Dom Odo Casel's "cult-mysterion" became "signs of love"; the technical epistemological language of Bernard Lonergan's *Insight* became "life-giving moments"; and Gene hit on the notion of "hospitality" as central to the first step in the liturgical action as well as the first step in human action. Gene teamed up with some new students — Elaine Rendler as a musical resource and John Buscemi as a visual artist — and he exchanged ideas with them in a number of settings. For his friends and associates Gene was father, grandfather, mentor, philosopher, raconteur and, most often, provocateur!

Gene wrote and rewrote, honing and polishing the ideas he discovered, and fit them together with truths he had experienced and principles he had espoused since his seminary teaching days. "Once you have found the first truth," he would say, "you are more likely to discover the second. Once you have the second, you are even more likely to find the third." In reading Gene's books, you are the beneficiary of fifty years of his work.

The task I was asked to take on in this essay was to "write about Gene's place in the liturgical-spiritual movement in the U.S." Up to this point, I have chronicled (somewhat autobiographically and historically) Gene's role in the liturgical movement. I have avoided speaking about the spiritual movement, because Gene as a spiritual director used a combination of nondirective psychology, confrontational challenge and common sense that was quite unique to his personality and to his effectiveness. At the beginning of each school year, there was always a waiting line of seminarians seeking him as a spiritual advisor, though he took only a limited number of students.

But beneath the uniquely personal aspects of his spiritual direction, as you have read in this book, Gene rejected the fundamental premise on which most "spiritualities" are based, that is, he rejected the division between spirit and matter, and therefore he rejected anything that smacked of a piety aimed at "dematerializing" the spiritual life. In its place, he argued for becoming fully human, stressing Joseph Pieper's position that leisure is the basis of culture and Jacques Maritain's position that contemplation is something everyone does; just as insight, for Lonergan, is something everyone has . . . but has to learn how to use.

I would like to conclude with a personal assessment of Gene's role in the liturgical movement in the United States. It is my own hypothesis that five major "styles" or "schools" of celebration have emerged since the Second Vatican Council.[8]

I call these styles *monastic, ritualistic, dramatic, small group* and *communicative*.

"Once you have found the first truth," he would say, "you are more likely to discover the second. Once you have the second, you are even more likely to find the third."

The *monastic style* grew from the practice at St. John's Abbey, Collegeville, Minnesota; it features a presider who asks the assembly to participate in otherworldly holiness. Its music is chant; its goal is to reveal a transcendent God.

The *ritualistic style* is expressed in the liturgical model embraced by the University of Notre Dame Center for Pastoral Liturgy; it features "smells (incense) and bells." Its music is hymnody, and its goal is to lead the assembly to a God who is faithful and dependable. (People who worship in this style always sit in the same seats at church.)

The *dramatic style* of liturgical celebration grew from the Jesuit Liturgical School in Berkeley, California; it features a presider who seeks to delight the assembly. Use of music, dance, drama and the creative arts can border on entertainment. The goal of this style is to reveal the God of beauty.

Small group celebrations are so influenced by the cohesiveness of the assembly that all of the ritual patterns and music are directly chosen to reinforce this cohesion. For instance, a group of people involved in social action who gather for the eucharist might choose to sing Tom Conry's music; a community deliberately celebrating African American or Hispanic roots might choose music deriving from and expressive of those traditions. The goal of such a celebration style is to lead the assembly to a God who acts and calls the members to action.

The *communicative style* of celebration features a celebrant who desires to make sure that the assembly understands what is taking place: meaning is central. "What you see is what you get." No magic, no pretense. The music of this school is dominated by melodies which carry the specific meaning of the text, such as Suzanne Toolan's "I Am the Bread of Life" (with its historically developing refrain, "And I will raise him/her/them/you up"), in which the meaning is so specific that assemblies singing this text at a funeral for a woman may insist on singing "her" in the refrain because they understand the "meaning" of the text. The purpose of this school is to communicate a God of meaning, in fact, a God of *accessible* meaning.

The principal proponent and definer of this school was Gene Walsh. So in addition to Gene's role as teacher and educator, in addition to the very specific role he played in the development of the liturgical renewal in the United States, through his lectures and writings Gene developed what has become one of the five major schools of liturgical celebration in the United States — and, in my opinion, the one which most reflects the thinking of the Second Vatican Council.

As you read his writings, I am sure that you will be struck with Gene's constant call for adult faith and adult worship. As I read the material, I hear echoes of a college professor encouraging 19- and 20-year-old seminarians to determine their sense of *arete*, their vision of what a developed human being should become. And the central themes remain the same:

> God first loves me.
>
> Humans must communicate in signs.
>
> Gather, listen, respond.
>
> Hospitality, active listening, act.
>
> You are as good a lover as you are a sign maker.

These realities are powerful. They can change you. They can change the world. Gene believed that. So do I.

---

[1] Walsh followed the thought of Werner Jaeger, who taught that central to the Greek idea of *arete,* or "excellence," was the aim of classical humanism to "make a man" rather than "develop the child."

[2] For a complete treatment see Virgil C. Funk, "The History of the Liturgical Movement" in *The New Dictionary of Sacramental Worship*, Peter Fink, S.J., editor (Collegeville: The Liturgical Press, 1992).

[3] The Liturgical Conference continues today as an ecumenical association dedicated to the renewal of the churches, especially through the renewal of worship.

[4] Eugene A. Walsh, *The Priesthood in the Writings of the French School: Berulle, De Condren, Olier* (Washington, DC: Catholic University of America Press, 1949).

[5] Dom Odo Casel was a Benedictine monk of Maria Laach Abbey in Germany.

[6] Along with Joseph Connolly of Baltimore, Omer Westendorf and Johannes Hofinger of New Orleans, Gene Walsh developed the notion of the four-hymn Mass.

[7] Timothy Leonard, *Geno: A Biography of Eugene Walsh, S.S.* (Washington, DC: The Pastoral Press, 1988) 145.

[8] See Virgil C. Funk, "Enculturation, Style and the Sacred-Secular Debate," in *Sacred Sound and Social Change,* Lawrence A. Hoffman and Janet R. Walton, editors (Notre Dame: University of Notre Dame Press, 1992) 314–22.

Virgil C. Funk, presbyter of the diocese of Richmond, Virginia, is founder and president of the National Association of Pastoral Musicians, an association of musicians dedicated to fostering the art of musical liturgy.